DATE DUE			

CHAIN CARVERS

CHAIN CARVERS

Old Men Crafting Meaning

SIMON J. BRONNER

THE UNIVERSITY PRESS OF KENTUCKY

Copyright © 1985 by The University Press of Kentucky

Scholarly publisher for the Commonwealth,
serving Bellarmine College, Berea College, Centre
College of Kentucky, Eastern Kentucky University,
The Filson Club, Georgetown College, Kentucky
Historical Society, Kentucky State University,
Morehead State University, Murray State University,
Northern Kentucky University, Transylvania University,
University of Kentucky, University of Louisville,
and Western Kentucky University.

Editorial and Sales Offices: Lexington, Kentucky 40506-0024

Library of Congress Cataloging in Publication Data

Bronner, Simon J.
    Chain carvers.

    Bibliography: p.
    Includes index.
        1. Wood-carvers—Indiana—Interviews. 2. Wood-
carving—Indiana—Psychological aspects. 3. Folk art—
Indiana—Psychological aspects. 4. Chains—Folklore.
I. Title.
NK9712.B75 1984   736'.4   84-11930
ISBN 0-8131-1523-X

To my "old man"—signed, Shimon Josef

CONTENTS

Preface

IN THIS book I tell of my conversations with several men who carve chains and other related objects. The linked chain cut from a single block of wood is the most persistent and universal form of wood-carving. I do not pretend to explain every global instance of chain carving; rather, I look at the experiences of a few carvers in one locale to see what patterns emerge. I especially argue that people often use creativity to help them adjust—sometimes to a new situation, a life crisis, or emotional conflicts and tensions.

The chain carvers I found turned out to be old men, often removed from their childhood rural homes to industrial surroundings. Retired, they had time on their hands, which they filled with wood, dust, and creativity. They had taken up a folk practice they remembered from childhood. To talk about their woodcarving is to talk about aging and masculinity, about social and economic change, but, mostly, about the carvers themselves and the craft they hold dear. I devote considerable space to the carvers' experiences as they and their neighbors described them to me, bringing out the motives and conditions that prompted their need for adjustment and creativity. Some will want to call my work psychological and folkloristic; I think of it as a personal approach that combines art, tradition, and behavior.

But why chains? Traditional forms like chains hold a special fascination for makers and viewers alike. The chain becomes a riddle that challenges categories of reality and imagination. Its ambiguity forces the viewer to think about the object and what it represents. The chain is playful and serious; it is art and craft; it draws attention to itself and to its maker. Chains commonly take on an affecting symbolism.

When people make things, they convey their hidden feelings, their grave concerns, and their cherished values. Objects are often the symbols that speak for us when words fail. The shapes our objects take, and how we build and use them, have meanings often outside our awareness, yet crucial to our perceptions of ourselves and the world around us. I stress the plural "meanings" because symbols found in the crafted object permit different translations into ideas by makers and viewers. Uncovering the symbolism, and its various meanings, gets at why we do and think what we do. Working from this premise, I explore the carvers' reasons for undertaking carving, their special ways of making and using objects, and the consequent perceptions of their actions and products.

When I first collected and organized my material years ago, I began talking about it before various civic and cultural organizations. The question most often put to me was, "Why do they do it?" After all, despite their visual and tactile appeal, carved chains could easily look to some a tedious, eccentric, outmoded thing to make. My questioners wanted the one quick capsule that would clear it all up, but it's not that simple. Different carvers have their own stories to tell. My task was to collate and interpret what the carvers meant, and implied. I also had to deal with public misconceptions about carving as a trifling hobby. I wrote this book to describe the many facets of chain carving and to set down some interpretations of this captivating practice.

The objects the men make are not whimsical or odd, as some previous collectors and curators would have us believe. Such authorities commonly never talked to carvers. To know the carvers is to know the deep significance that making things has in their lives. Carved chains, commonly attached to hooks and caged balls, raise eyebrows wherever I show them, but from the consideration of the meanings and behavior behind them, I want to provoke thinking about other, often less striking, ways people insist on creativity to help them cope.

The behavior that surrounds a creative act is observable and commonly unselfconscious. I worry that most craft studies neglect the behavior of makers and viewers of things, in favor of a narrow look at the finished objects. Carvers themselves talk readily about their finished wares but less easily about what they did while, and before, making them. In the silent concentration that directs the movement of the fingers, the hunch of the shoulders; even in the sudden breaking from work, messages are transmitted. Close observation of behavior, of habit and ritual, may reveal more at some points about the state of mind of the creator than could words. In chronicling actions, as well as recording words and looking at the finished objects, I suggest that studying behavior, the *doing* of a craft, is an effective way for the student of culture to get at thought and idea—at mind.

Chain carving is far from trivial for talking about behavior and mind. Thinking about getting old, worrying about being unappreciated, coping with rapid social change—these are some of the fundamental problems that the chain carvers I met confronted. Their creativity and folk knowledge—picked up through word of mouth, imitation, demonstration, and custom—helped them. Leaning on tradition, yet making sure their objects had their personal marks, the men found in chain carving something tangible, to reach deep within themselves and to outwardly touch and move others.

These men are not alone. Other people choose different expressions of informal learning. Often, I hear women talk about the emotional problems worked out, or at least set aside, during quilting or baking. Children, too, have their self-satisfying, symbolic practices. The things they make, like fortune-telling devices made out of folded paper, playfully deal with the uncertainty of the future. As children, and even more it seems as adults, it becomes important for us to decorate the spaces in which we live and work with personal mementos and reminders of our identity. Whatever the expression, it signifies the need people have for creativity, especially the kind that taps and alters traditional forms. The humanist in all of us should seek the wellspring of this creativity, this striking, but often overlooked, enactment of skill and need for beauty in everyday lives.

This book describes a humble form of woodcarving, which has thus far evaded the watchful eyes of cultural critics, to reveal a view of the men who practice it and the society of which they are a part. In the prologue, I describe the beginnings of my research and the substantial history of chain carving. Where is it found? How old is it? How did it come to the United States? Sifting the many bits and pieces of evidence, I was left with parts of a puzzle. I put them together to present an idea of chain carving's connections to the past, to bring you up to the present when I came across my first chain carvers in southern Indiana. The epilogue contains my reflections on the carvers and their creations as I closed my research. In between, the book's three chapters speak their themes through titles taken from the carvers' own words. In "Part of You is in a Carving. . . . " I discuss the carvers' experiences as they bear on their woodcarving. "Bet You Don't Know How I Made This" is about the techniques of chain carving. How is it made? With what materials? What's the trick to it anyway? The final chapter "How Do You Figure It, That Darn Stuff?"—presents my interpretations of chain carving's meanings. It was carver George Blume, more than eighty years old, who challenged me to explain "that darn stuff," chain carving, which had been an important part of his life. I hope I figured it right (George thought so).

I have many people to thank for helping me complete this work. Professor Warren Roberts of Indiana University at Bloomington lent his guidance early, and his wisdom and encouragement continue to inspire me. The Rockefeller Foundation made my research possible by funding the bulk of my study from 1978 to 1981. The Pennsylvania State University granted me invaluable assistance and funding to complete my research in 1982. I also appreciate the less tangible, but nonetheless valuable, support I received from the staffs of Humanities and Behavioral Sciences at the Pennsylvania State University's Capitol Campus. Their interest kept me going.

I also benefited from the helpful extended "family" of folklorists and American Studies professionals. I want to acknowledge the counsel of Michael Owen Jones, Ronald L. Baker, Marsha MacDowell, C. Kurt Dewhurst, Ken Ames, Louis C. Jones, John Michael Vlach, William K. McNeil, William Ferris, Deb Bowman, Elliott Oring, William Wilson, Wilhelm Nicolaisen, Barbara Kirshenblatt-Gimblett, Henry Glassie, Roger Mitchell, Shalom Staub, Yvonne Milspaw, Don Yoder, Ken Thigpen, Dan Ward, and Howard Marshall. At Indiana University I felt a special fondness for my stimulating days of discussion at the Folklore Institute with John Hasse, Sandra Stahl, Richard Dorson, William Wiggins, Stephen Stern, Catherine Swanson, Doris Fanelli, Robert Fanelli, Thomas A. Adler, Elizabeth Mosby Adler, Gary Stanton, Priscilla Denby, Tom Walker, and Stephen Poyser. Robert Gunderson and George Juergens from American Studies and Brigid O'Hanrahan from Art were equally inspiring. They will be heartened to know, though, that I take sole responsibility for the opinions in this book.

For their help in the field, I extend my gratitude to Lil Blemker,

Carol Blemker, Alice Morrison, Egle Žygas, Kathleen Mundell, Susan Johnson, and, again, Warren Roberts. For their aid in the arduous task of transcription, I offer my special thanks to Peter Voorheis and Tina Bucuvalas. Darrell Peterson graciously lent his photographic expertise, Cynthia Barry gave her valued editorial advice, Kathy LaTulippe brought her graphic skill, and Theresa Vilcheck, as her name coincidentally implies, helped check the manuscript. For her special care and patience with clerical matters, I send every possible compliment to Kathy Ritter, the steady rock of the office.

I must have been difficult to live with during the last stages of the work (then again, some friends think I'm difficult even when I'm not working). So for their tolerance and concern, I thank my Harrisburg, Pennsylvania, friends, especially Pam deWall, Frederick Richmond, John Teske, Harry Spector, Betsy McKinstry, Susan Kogan, Beebe Frazer, Irwin Richman, Charles Townley, Michael Barton, John Patterson, and, I hasten to add, the Old World Folk Band. East Lansing, Michigan, lingers in my heart too. During my all-too-brief stay at Michigan State University, I was gifted with the caring of many people, especially Clare MacDowell and her family, and Martha Brownscombe. I feel fortunate to have been with such keen minds and willing ears in the places I have worked.

Most of all, I will always be indebted to the carvers and to their families and friends, who gave me their time and attention. In the years ahead I shall continue to cherish their kindness and teaching. This book is for them, and others like them.

ILLUSTRATION CREDITS

Photographs are by Simon Bronner and drawings are by Kathy LaTulippe, except as indicated, by page number, below:

xiv Simon Bronner. 2, 37 Elliott Oring. 11 Indiana University Museum. 13 Greenfield Village and the Henry Ford Museum. 14 Chuck and Jan Rosenak Collection; photo by Breger & Associates. 44, 54 Simon Bronner Collection. 77 Jim Sargent & Jim Schleyer, *Pocket Price Guide: W.R. Case & Sons Pocket Knives,* copyright 1982 by Knife Nook. 110 Jeanne S. Morgan. 111 Michael Owen Jones. 112 Horydczak Collection, Library of Congress; reprinted with permission of Russell Sage Foundation and Library of Congress. 148 Universal Pictures. 151 Hershey Museum of American Life. 155 Darrell Peterson.

Part of you is in a carving, see;
there's something there that goes with it.
FLOYD BENNINGTON

MICHIGAN

OHIO

INDIANA

KANSAS

INDIANAPOLIS

BLOOMINGTON

SOLSBERRY

ILLINOIS

PLAINVILLE

JASPER

HUNTINGBURG

SIBERIA

LOUISVILLE

ST PHILIP

KENTUCKY

0   20   40 miles

FAIRPLAY

Prologue

My map didn't tell me where I was as much as the corn fields suspiciously looking over my shoulder, and just in front of me, homespun German-signed mailboxes waiting attentively. Stuck in rusted milkcans, the mailboxes were emblems of a German-American heritage combined with midwestern "down on the farm" spirit. The old barns and bucolic Catholic churches scattered throughout the area showed tradition's weathered persistence here. This was southwestern Indiana, around Dubois (pronounced Do-Boys) County. I was headed toward Adyeville on the advice of an Indiana University professor who told me of a curious collection of carvings.

I pulled up at a remote and tattered barn serving as an antique store, or junk shop, depending on your point of view. The owner had a collection of old farm equipment—several well-aged tractors and implements—exposed to the hot, humid Indiana summer. A portly old man in overalls welcomed me in a German accent capped with a Hoosier twang.

"Vat you lookin' fer?"

"Do you have some woodcarvings made by a local man?" I asked.

"Oh, you mean tem chains and tings? Ya, they're sometin', all right. Come on in, but I'm not selling tem. I've gotten used to 'em. They're my company sometimes."

My curiosity aroused, I climbed the rickety steps to find a table piled with wooden houses, barns, churches, tools, figures, and furniture—all obviously handcarved. Several long wooden chains, some complete with wooden swivels, joints, caged balls, and hooks, were draped from the rafters.

"Who made this?" I asked.

"Some old guy in Huntingburg. . . . He's probably dead now, ya.

George Blume's carvings on display in the barn

He couldn't carve anymore and he needed sometin' to live on, so I took 'em."

I left, nagged by questions. Who was this man? Was he still around? Why would he make these things? How did he do it anyway?

At my lodgings, I met a woman who gave me the name of someone who might know this carver. I drove to Huntingburg the next day to meet Lil Blemker. She was a long-time resident of the area and sharply attuned to its traditions. It didn't take me long to feel close to Lil. She was warm, gracious, and motherly.

She thought aloud about the character of the area. "This place still has lots of old-timers to learn from, but the times are changing you know. The kids don't stay; the place has grown up different. The place has tradition all right, but it has grown up different."

I broached the subject of the woodcarvings I had seen, and she surprised me by offering to take me to him. "Why he's out on his porch every day this time of year," she explained.

Sure enough, there he was.

"Howdy, yeah my name is George Blume (pronounced Bloom-ee). You're from Bloomington? That's like the other side of the moon, yep. Probably named after me though, hah hah. . . . You see them things I made, huh? That's darn stuff, ain't it? Yep, like them chains. My daughter has one yet. What do you want to know?"

We talked for hours. Usually I had to yell because of his hearing loss. I must have been quite a sight screaming questions with tape recorder at my feet and camera tugging at my neck. But I couldn't have asked for a more willing informant. Day after day I sat on his cramped porch, taking notes and trying to keep cool, while he, oblivious to the heat, told me at length about his life and carvings—and especially his favored chains.

George was past eighty. His hands shook. His eyes faltered. But his spirit was strong. He couldn't carve anymore, but he wanted to relive making them by talking about them. He sat on his porch waiting for people to listen. Few came. He lived in a room in his daughter's house. The room was surprisingly bare for a man who had made so many things in his life. Vitamins and pills lined the top of his dresser; his walls looked stark. When I visited he would bring small items out to me: a wooden dart he made as a child; a whimmy-diddle (a wooden stick with grooves cut in, which, when rubbed with another piece of wood, amazingly moved a propeller on the end of

George with twenty-foot chain he gave to his daughter

the stick); an outline of a fat chain link drawn into a block of wood. George drew me close to him and his craft, and I wondered if there were others around who made such things.

A friend working in the area told me to visit Floyd Bennington, who lived only a few blocks away from George. Floyd took me to his den where I saw carved chains and caged balls displayed proudly beneath his family pictures. The carvings were small and delicate, and I noticed that Floyd himself was a small man with delicate

Floyd Bennington with his chain and caged ball

features. He had a regal smile and a caring face. His hands showed wear from many years of working with knives and woods. The roughness of his hands stood in sharp contrast to the polish and detail of his small objects.

Well into his seventies, Floyd had energy that defied his age. He paused in our conversation to help his invalid wife. She was proud of his achievements and encouraged him to bring his carving tools into the living room. Smiling broadly, he went through the steps of

Willie Hausmann's chain displayed in the home
of the Reverend Ken Scherry

carving a chain and caged ball with the clarity and patience of a teacher. When I complimented him, he laughed and told me that he had taught for almost fifty years, many of them in one-room schoolhouses. Carving was not something he coldly taught, but something very much a part of his learning and experience.

Floyd, in turn, told me to visit the Reverend Ken Scherry in downtown Huntingburg. Floyd's eyes sparkled as he said, "He has something you'll want to see."

In Scherry's house, the first thing I noticed was a seven-foot wooden chain hanging majestically across his fireplace. It had delicate anchors, hearts, and tightly caged balls hanging from the links. The chain commanded the attention of anyone in the living room.

"Yes, I like that stuff, but I didn't make it," Scherry explained. "A parishioner down in St. Philip, Indiana—Willie Hausmann's his name—made it for me as a token of friendship. Made it out of one block of wood, with no glue . . . just a pocketknife!"

Hausmann had died a few years back. Scherry showed me a picture of him on his front porch, carved cane in hand and pet raccoon at his feet.

"After his wife died," Scherry told me, "I would walk into his kitchen and it would be knee-high in woodshavings. He'd be there whittling away at those chains. Made 'em for relatives and friends. Kept him busy, all right."

I wrote down the names of Willie Hausmann's surviving relatives and made the trip to St. Philip, just west of Evansville in the southwestern corner of the state. Ed Hausmann, Willie's cousin, invited me in and described woodworking traditions that extended beyond Willie to other residents in the area. The list of names grew; notes filled my pads quickly.

The summer drew to a close, and I headed back home to Bloomington, some seventy miles north of Dubois County. I thought my fieldwork was over, but, almost in my own backyard, I stumbled upon chain-carver Wandley Burch. He was at a crafts festival in the courthouse square, giving away small wooden pliers "made out of one piece of wood." I made arrangements to go to his home on the west side of town.

Sitting in Wandley's kitchen having coffee, I eyed a wooden chain hanging beside framed photographs of the family and the old homestead. Wandley took me down to his dark basement, where a

Wandley Burch with his chain and caged ball

cramped workshop held shelves filled with carved chains, pliers, crowns, caged balls, and canes. Long and lanky, Wandley had to stoop to get around his packed basement. A rugged face complemented his rough-hewn carvings. His age drew well-worn wrinkles in his face and bleached his hair a harsh white. But his hands reached out with gentleness and an air of southern leisureliness. That idle air was deceiving, though, for he was the most productive carver I had met. Every day was filled with carving more and giving away more. He liked "visiting," people dropping in to chat. I wandered in often, catching him roughing out a three- or four-foot length of chain. The coffee was always hot, and I stirred up many questions.

Earnest Bennett working on a chain

Shortly after I met Wandley, an Indianapolis friend, knowing of my growing collection of chains (the bad jokes I endured were worth the tips I received), led me to Earnest Bennett on the north side of the city. His carvings lay on a table in his bedroom. His chains stood out, because they improvised on the basic theme with flair and precision. Wooden snakes and belt buckles wrapped around smooth links; joints and swivels made improbable connections. Although playful, the carvings were also controlled, masterly. Multiple balls sat caged behind a series of even bars, Earnest their crafty jailer.

Earnest's workshop was sunnier, more open, and more organized than Wandley's. Earnest moved about his spacious house pointing to the things he had made and bringing up the places he had been. Born more than seventy-five years earlier in an isolated pocket of Kentucky, Earnest had traveled around the world yet had never lost sight of his roots. Carving brought him back home.

More leads followed, and I quickly realized that chain carving is neither strictly regional nor ethnic—common but usually unwarranted cubbyholes into which folk crafts are sometimes classified. Chain carving belongs to many people in diverse walks of life. A common thread? Consistently I came across carvers who were elderly men. But I wanted to know by what means chain carving had reached these men. Where else in the world is chain carving practiced? How old is it? How did it get to southern Indiana? Who usually made chains? For what purpose? Would the wooden chain's past tell me more about the present?

I checked museums; I read woodcarving books; I called collectors. I hoped to discover a sharp picture, to uncover a single point of origin from which chain carving had come to America, but I had to admit to a hazy sketch. Part of the problem lay in the sources. Books boasted slick photographs of carvings set against sterile backgrounds. The background was lost indeed. Collectors stressed the styles and types of chains. The maker, date, and place of origin of the chains were often not recorded or were unknown. From what I could tell, though, chain carving was widespread throughout the world and had been around for a long time.

In Scandinavia, as early as the Viking era, carvers made decorative wooden spoons with chains as love tokens or demonstrations of skill. In fourteenth-century France, a carved chain was used as a girdle. In Wales love spoons with chains, dating from the seventeenth century, are found and there are also some traces of chain carving in eighteenth- and nineteenth-century England, Scandinavia, and Switzerland. European examples often had caged balls, anchors, and hooks—designs also common in New World chains. European carvers also included chains and caged balls in knitting sheaths, yarn winders, cheese scoops, canes, and lace bobbins. European men probably made these highly decorated objects as love tokens for women.[1]

In Africa, ethnographers documented—among the Tsonga, Venda, and Nguni tribes—twin headrests connected with chains carved

Egyptian chain and rings-on-shaft, ca. 1970

out of one block of wood. The dates of these examples are uncertain, but folklorist William Wiggins described an active chain carver in Liberia who told him that the tradition of carving such "love chains" reaches back many generations. Another folklorist, John Vlach, located caged balls in Africa similar to ones he had found in Georgia. He suggested that such carvings could be continuous with African tradition.[2]

In the Middle East, Asaad Nadim found in 1975 that for many years young Egyptian arabesque carpenters had carved wooden chains and chains-on-shafts to prove their skill to their peers and elders. Farther north in Slavic countries, researchers came across wooden-chain carvings on spoons, spinning wheels, and drawing pins. In eastern Asia, art historians identified chains and caged balls made of solid blocks of ivory and nephrite. Marian and Charles Klamkin speculated that chain carving originated in China, but they lacked evidence and could not develop their contention.[3]

In North America, chain carving has been present among European settlers since colonial times. Surviving chain carvings made by

European settlers in America, however, generally lack the elaborate ornamentation of European antecedents. Old American chain carvings usually contain a small wooden length of chain with a simple caged ball, spoon, or hook. Apparently, the predominant European use of chains for love tokens was not as common in America. Early American settlers from Europe seem to have carved chains as demonstrations of skill and as objects of decoration.[4]

Researchers often listed chain carving as part of the cultural repertoire of various ethnic groups in America. They found carved chains among French-Canadians, German-Canadians, and Alaskan Eskimos. Among Afro-Americans, researchers documented modern instances of wooden-chain carving in Tennessee and Georgia, and recorded at least one black-made example from 1790.[5] Let's assume, then, that wooden-chain carving was probably disseminated in America by its European and African immigrants.

As settlers from the Carolinas and Virginia flowed west into Kentucky and southern Indiana, did they bring a knowledge of chain carving with them?[6] There is some evidence that they did. I have been able to locate Indiana chains and caged balls dating back into the nineteenth century. The Wayne County Historical Museum in Richmond, Indiana, has caged balls made in 1870 by a Cambridge City youth of German extraction. The Indianapolis Children's Museum has eleven chains with caged balls made by a local carver around 1860. Collectors also report chain carvings from around the same time along the route of southern migration to Indiana.[7]

The nineteenth century witnessed a large wave of German settlement in Indiana. George Blume, Ed Hausmann, Alois Schuch, and Leo Klueh—southern Indiana informants of German ancestry— described to me chain carving among German-born settlers in their grandparents' generation. Art historian Charles van Ravenswaay wrote that Germans who entered Missouri in the nineteenth century brought with them many woodcarvings and wood-carving skills, although he did not mention chains specifically. Recently, however, the William Penn Memorial Museum in Harrisburg, Pennsylvania, displayed the work of John Scholl, a woodcarver born in Germany in 1827 and raised there, who settled in Germania, Pennsylvania. He carved chains and caged balls until his death in 1926.[8] Also spanning the nineteenth and twentieth centuries are the elaborate chains and caged balls that Pennsylvania-German David Strausser left to the

Hershey Museum of American Life. Did they bear connections or similarities to German woodcarvers who entered southern Indiana in the nineteenth century? We can't really be sure (just as we can't be sure of the influence of blacks and Indians on the early history of American woodcarving), but the evidence shows that at least some European settlers in the different waves of migration brought chain carving to southern Indiana.

Hobos, sailors, peddlers, and migrant workers also helped spread chain carving. Leo Klueh of Ferdinand, in Dubois County, Indiana, learned how to make wooden pliers out of one piece of wood from a hobo. Victor Schutz of Jasper remembered hobos selling him carved canes with caged balls. Writer Steven Banks argued that sailors for centuries used their free time, often abundant, to carve wood—among other materials—and that they spread this knowledge to fellow sailors and landlubbers alike. He reported several chains and caged balls on love spoons and knitting sheaths made by sailors in the eighteenth and nineteenth centuries.[9] The Mystic Seaport Museum in Connecticut adds to the evidence by reporting a bookcase in their collections with caged balls signed by a sailor from Massachusetts in 1861.[10] Conceivably, the early prevalence of shipping on America's coast brought with it the distribution of decorative objects made by sailors.

Ed Hausmann still has wooden chains, puzzles, and caged balls made before World War I by a migrant worker on the Hausmann farm in St. Philip, Indiana. Willie Hausmann learned to carve such objects from this man, and Willie's family told me that other migrant workers who came to the area frequently carved between jobs. Chain carving is also reported among lumbermen and other woodworkers. In Michigan and Oregon, for example, lumbermen whittled chains to pass time and show off their skill.[11]

Thus, we can say that chain carving is or has been

Cane with caged ball carved by logger James Marshall Foster of Watersmeet, Michigan, ca. 1906

practiced throughout the world, mainly by men, and has persisted for several centuries. Immigrants from Europe and slaves from Africa were the primary means by which wooden chain carving entered America. In southern Indiana, wooden-chain carving continues into the present and shows strong signs of enduring. Elsewhere, too, from Maine to Oregon, Carolina to California, I hear of traditional carvers. The carvers work both in clubs and alone, on the farm and in the city.

The basic forms and materials of chain carving have generally remained stable. An exception is the elaborate love spoon and knitting sheath from Europe, which did not catch on in America. New types of chain making also appear. I have found references to chains made of stone and large logs (cut with a chainsaw), and I have watched gum-wrapper chains and pop-top chains made by adolescents to "pass time" or to act as "love tokens" and divining devices.[12]

Although I had established the existence of a long-standing tradition of chain carving, that did little to explain why the men I met took it up. I tried asking the carvers, but the answers didn't come easily. It was too close to them. They told me instead of their lives, their experiences, their hopes and frustrations. The answers lay hidden behind the words, emotions, and actions of the carvers. I had to listen and watch more closely.

I returned to Huntingburg the following summer. The men I had met earlier claimed to have led undistinguished lives, but, in fact, the stories they told of their lives and skills and of problems confronted through creativity deserved distinction. George Blume, Floyd Bennington, Wandley Burch, and Earnest Bennett became the mainstays of my interest. I was determined to know them and, through them, understand the creative impulse and traditional underpinnings of chain carving.

Lil and Ike Blemker took me into their home my second summer in Dubois County. When I went to visit

Chain made by Larry Stinson, Bethesda, Maryland, ca. 1930

the carvers, it was as someone who "was from nearby." I had more time to listen and to look. The carvings I saw took on a new significance, for I was learning about the human story and struggle behind their making.

One day in the barn that held George Blume's carvings, I saw something I had not noticed previously. Tucked away in a corner of the table was lettering cut into wood. It read "Home Sweet Home." I remembered George mentioning it now, and how he missed its smell and feel. Pushed aside and aged, yet so expressive, the sign read poignantly. As I stood staring at the table in the barn's dim light, children and their parents were stopping to look at the wooden carvings. A child reached out to touch a hanging chain.

"Don't touch!" his mother admonished.

"But I want to see how it's done," the little boy shot back. "Do you know how those links are put together?"

Mom wished she knew. Pushing the child along, she turned to me with a questioning glance. "Why would someone do all that?"

I smiled. "I'm asking that too. I intend to find out."

George Blume holding
his carved pliers

CHAPTER ONE

Part of You
Is in a Carving

"WHERE had the time gone?" I thought. My watch ticked impatient-
ly. It was late, but I didn't want to leave. George Blume was speaking fast, in his usual staccato fashion, of a time he remembered when
a man had to make everything from tools to toys, for himself. Suddenly, George noticed the dark around us. With disappointment in
his voice, he said, "Well, I guess you'd best be going."

I nodded and began packing my gear. I had my arms full when
I heard him think aloud to himself.

"Yeah, that reminds me, yes sir, when I would make them things.
I did a lot of baloney, all right. I went through a lot of bull and I made
a lot of bull . . . yeah, a lot of bull."

I stopped and listened.

In no chronological order and in no apparent logical pattern, out
cascaded a verbal stream of past incidents that marked for him the
flow of his life. Looking back more than eighty years, he ordered his
experiences and accomplishments by talking to me. I had asked him
to unveil his past the way no friend or relative had. Doing so brought
out much of his inner self, more than he had ever revealed before.
He said he was glad for that, but I thought it made him anxious too.
When I said we would talk again tomorrow, he chuckled and responded, "Yeah, I'll have more lies for you by then."

His laughter suggested to me that, indeed, the truthfulness of
what he told me surprised him, maybe disturbed him too. His life
was subtly etched into his creations, and I had brought his creations

and life back into view. Knowing what came to his mind when he recounted the connections between his experience and his creativity let me into his world and the world he tried to make in wood.

Floyd Bennington and I were talking in his living room, he having spread photos of his pioneering ancestors and their houses before me. Then came the shots of one-room schoolhouses where he had begun teaching and the sprawling central school where he had ended his career. The continuity of his life with families past and future emerged. I photographed him in front of his "family wall," a whole side of a den bragging of family portraits. He held up a wooden chain and caged ball from a table below the portraits for the camera to preserve.

"Can you get them?" Floyd said with concern, motioning to the wooden creations in his outstretched palms.

Floyd showed me his latest project in the garage-turned-woodworking shop. Here he was lord; the tools and paints answered only to him. We returned to the living room where he sat back on the sofa and reminisced. His wife seemed amused by the scene. Floyd's fingers moved over his pocketknife as we talked. He placed a wooden chain he was completing on the table between us, and I could sense his past surging before me.

Floyd spoke more deliberately than the other carvers. His eyes drifted off when he talked. He punctuated his thoughts with broad smiles and smooth waves of the hand. When he drew on his memory, he sought order. He sorted the jumble of events in his life into a successive line. Just when I thought he was engrossed in his own thoughts, he would cock his head and look deep into my eyes. He spoke with directness, but deeper within were many stray thoughts looking for definition.

Wandley Burch spent much time talking to me in his basement workshop. He would frequently pick up wooden chains or pliers and bounce them in his hand.

"Here, take that," he would say as he put the thing in my hand.

"But . . . ," I would object.

"Go ahead, put it in your pocket."

There was no arguing. The objects were part of the conversation. They told him that he reached me, and they reminded me that I was there and had listened. Wandley spoke softly in a hard Hoosier mumble. He was often most serious when he was trying to kid. He

would cackle ever so briefly, as if taking it back, when he realized
that a joking remark rubbed hard at the truth. His voice lacked much
variation, but it showed mood easily. He talked most fluidly when
around his things strewn in the basement: old books, machinery, carvings, tools, and lots of wood.

"That anvil over there is my dad's, you know."

His mind raced back. "Yeah, you know I came to Indiana in a
covered wagon. My dad, he. . . ."

We moved back to the living room, and his wife, always in good
cheer despite a bad hip that gave her pain, would join in with
memories and encouragement for Wandley.

As I made my goodbyes with nods and handshakes, I was left awed
by Wandley's large, commanding hands. I thought back to the assured
way he grasped his carvings in those rough palms and the gentle, expressive way he put them in mine. The carvings often spoke for him.
At the door, Wandley arched his back, curled his brow, and smiled.

"I'll be here when you get back, uh huh. I'll be doing more
whittling. . . ."

As I drove to Earnest Bennett's home on the outskirts of Indianapolis, I could see old barns fighting for life in the shadow of the
highway. In Earnest's mind, this was farm country lost to the city.
Earnest's house, like Floyd Bennington's, was a one-story, modern,
suburban affair. Yet inside was a man who spent much of his time
carving tiny replicas of old tools and things in rustic woods.

A quiet, peaceful man, Earnest wouldn't stand out in a crowd,
unless, of course, he had his carvings. His carvings have color, spirit,
flair. He kept them in his bedroom where they greeted him and his
wife when they awoke and sent them to sleep at night. Outside the
window was a lush garden, more evidence of Earnest's handiwork.

I told Earnest that I had tried to carve a chain from his instruc-
tions but that I had little to show for it except cuts in my hands. He
took me to his workshop and went through the subtleties of chain
carving again. Behind him was a wall full of neatly hung old tools
and instruments—a reminder of old values and old times, of past
places and pioneers. In this setting, he reflected on his life. His manner of speech was terse; his comments wise. Of all the carvers, he
said the least, but I often thought he conveyed the most. He pulled
from the wall a fretless, homemade banjo made by an elder relative
from his old Kentucky home, and asked me to play it. I gingerly

fingered the neck, while Earnest looked eagerly on. When I played it, the instrument resounded with back porches and times past. Earnest recorded it, and said, "Well, now we have tapes of each other!" It was his way of exchanging skills and sharing bonds with another generation.

When the carvers talked, I tried to draw out experiences that would help me interpret their carvings. "Part of you is in a carving," Floyd Bennington stressed, and his words rang true for the other carvers. To give some structure to the men's narratives, I specified dates and places: When were you born? Where? When did you move? Where again? When did you retire? When did you start carving? The answers gave bare outlines, but the picture started to get filled in when they rambled about themselves.

Even as I came to understand what was unique about each of the men, I recognized that George Blume, Floyd Bennington, Wandley Burch, and Earnest Bennett were not unlike the other carvers I met. I spotlight these four because they are the chaincarvers I know best, they live in the same general locale, and their experiences exemplify both the similar and diverse motives and conditions that can spark chain carving. Elderly, usually retired, and originally from the country, each tells of passing time by carving chains and other objects. They typically never sold their chains, but rather gave them to friends and relatives. They learned how to carve chains in childhood from a neighbor, uncle, father, or grandfather but picked it up again only after retirement or in old age. At some point they spent most of their time carving.

The rest of this chapter presents their stories. They are similar and different, joyful and tragic. The stories unfold in the order I met these men. I open with George too because his story extends more than the others, and he sets the stage more fully for the other dramas in the chapter. George's story is also the one most set in the past. On the other end Earnest's is most set in the present. Earnest is the most publicly active carver, although Wandley is probably the most productive. Floyd's tale bridges the others because he is more active now than George, but less so than Wandley and Earnest. He is the most reserved carver, but he also is the most philosophical.

Every man is his own historian, although often unintentionally. A man recalls incidents and lore that strike him as telling. When I came along I recorded those incidents and lore couched in running narratives of men's lives. I wasn't producing the often deceiving objectivity of biography, but the personal, subjective document of experience. The occasional folklore lacing the men's conversation—conspicuous stories, anecdotes, and sayings—offered autobiography in code. When the men couldn't talk about what values and visions they had, their folklore did. When surface facts of places and dates failed to order their personal history, elaborated accounts of events brought out hidden messages with the profoundness of feeling and involvement. What I present here, then, is a narrative embroidery framing the lives of the men. You'll find experiences and expressions weaving together values and creativity.

GEORGE'S STORY

Witches, Old-Timers, and Machines

George Blume has not carved for several years. Now in his eighties, he gardens in the morning and in the afternoon sits on his small front porch. Stationed in his favorite chair, he observes events in his quiet Huntingburg neighborhood, reads the paper, and occasionally talks to visitors.

"He loves to talk," Lil Blemker told me, but few visitors come around these days, because his friends, in George's words, "all kicked the bucket and went to heaven." He smiles as he says it, but the euphemism barely hides his thoughts.

He would lecture me on staying healthy. "You take these vitamins, you hear? Chew your pills, don't swallow them. Take an aspirin every day. Don't listen to them doctors. You're young yet." I was less than one-third his age when I began visiting George. He seemed eager to have company and to teach me about the "old stuff."

George Blume was born on a farm outside Schnellville, Dubois County, Indiana, on January 21, 1898, into a German-Catholic family of ten children. A year later, his father moved off the farm to open a general store six miles south in tiny Siberia. As a youth, George learned woodworking and farming from his father and grandfather.

George married in 1917. He worked his own farm near Siberia for five years. Drawn by the promise of higher wages, he settled in industrializing Huntingburg to work in a furniture factory. He stayed in Huntingburg, working at the same furniture factory almost forty years, and raised several children.

Around the time of his wife's death in 1959 he began carving chains and caged balls, forms familiar to him from his childhood. In the next few years he made carvings of tools, toys, buildings, and characters reminiscent of his rural experience. Failing eyesight and arthritis forced him to give up his carving around 1972, and shortly afterward he moved to his daughter's home. To give him extra money his daughter sold his carvings, numbering almost a thousand pieces, to their present home in Adyeville.

That's the outline of his story, but what were the influences on him, the memories he had that fill in the picture?

George's German background was important, for one. The area around Schnellville and Siberia where he grew up had a strong German-Catholic stamp. George's parents and neighbors spoke German exclusively. Priests held church services in German, and residents maintained German customs that George remembered well, such as "shooting in the New Year." On New Year's Eve, young bachelors from the town would ride to farmhouses and shoot off guns and create a ruckus. The farmer would obligingly come out to invite the bachelors in for a snack and toddy. Sometimes the young men would recite a verse or perform a skit in exchange. Then they would be off to the next farmhouse, and the next, until fatigue or drink would force them home. "Now, of course," George said slowly, "you don't have that anymore."

George's grandparents, born and bred in Germany, lived with the family. George's grandfather, Casper Blume, had a strong influence on George, although he died in 1906, when George was only eight years old. Casper spent long hours with George telling him stories about life in Germany. Casper trained George's hand in farming and old-time music making.

George's eyes glistened when he talked about his grandfather. When I asked George to give me an example of grandfather's stories, he responded with a dramatic narrative of witches and unusual events.

"My grandpa had a piece of ground in the bottom, and one day they had five hundred dollars laying in the house. In those days that was a lot of money.

"They were working one day in the bottom and Grandma says, 'Say Grandpa, there's somebody up at the house. You hear that dog barking up there? He don't bark unless there's somebody around.'

"Grandpa says, 'Don't worry about it. We can't go up there now. They know we're down here now. If they need us that badly they'll come down here.'

"And in the evening when they went home, the window in the kitchen was open. They got suspicious.

" 'How that window got open? We had it shut,' Grandma says. Grandma she went to the safe where the five hundred dollars was at. The five hundred dollars was gone. Grandpa said, 'Well, I'll be doggone, where's the five hundred dollars?!'

"So he went over to a neighbor who was one of these witchcraft people you know—help people get stuff back like that.

"Grandpa told the man, 'We were over there in the bottom yesterday. By golly, we heard our dog barking by the house, but we never made nothing out of it. Yesterday evening our window was laying open back in the kitchen and our five hundred dollars that had lain in the safe was gone. Can you do anything about it?'

" 'Sure,' the man said. 'I can get that money back for you if you want it.'

"Grandpa said, 'I sure would like to get it back.'

" 'Do you want to see the man to bring it back or do you just want your money back?'

"Grandpa said, 'I just want that money back, 'cause if I see the man I'll have a grudge against the man the rest of my days, so if you can, just get the money back.'

"They lit out to the barn, took a wagon wheel off a wagon, and planted a big spike in a tree. They put the wagon wheel on there, and the man said, 'Get back now.' They got to turn that wagon wheel there and went to mumbling something.

" 'How about it, do you want to see the man?'

" 'No, I don't want to see the man!'

" 'Well, your money will be back tomorrow morning. Just where it's at I can't tell you but it'll be back.'

"My grandpa went on home. Next morning he got up. He had to go down to the barn. He had to go through a big gate there with great big posts on the side. He went ahead on through the gate. The gate flopped shut. He thought he heard something fall or drop. Something laying there. He looked around; there's a path there on the other side. He looked and said, 'Well I'll be doggone, that's my money!'

"The man had said, 'Whatever money the man spent out of that, I can't get that back for you, but the money that he's got yet, I'll get that back for you.' I believe that fifteen dollars was spent out of it. That went by witchcraft, see there."[1]

"What other kinds of things would this witchcraft person do?" I asked.

"Those witchcraft people do anything. I was told one time by my grandpa. These priests got to learn that witchcraft. The last year they go to school, they got to learn that.

"Over there at Siberia there's a man. He was a good farmer and he had brothers. And by golly, all at once that good farmer and the brothers got mad at each other. And the good farmer had a bunch of cattle, and they started dying. They brought the doctor. Couldn't find nothing wrong with them. Told the farmer, 'I wouldn't know what's causing them cattle to die.'

"So by gosh, the farmer went to the priest. 'Say, I don't know but I think I've been witched. Can you do anything about it?'

" 'No,' said the priest. 'There ain't no such a thing; there ain't no such a thing. Forget that!'

" 'Well what's the cause of my cattle dying? I had a doctor look at that stuff and he say 'I can't find nothing out.'

" 'Now who do you think could be doing it?'

" 'I don't think it's anybody else but my brother. He's mad at me. I know he's doing stuff like that; he's got a book, a witchcraft book.'

"Priest said, 'Well just forget about it.'

"In the morning they took a buggy up to Uniontown. They rode up to a man's house. Priest said 'Say, Mister, I'd like to talk with you a little bit.'

"A man came out, and said 'What do you want to talk about?'

" 'Say, do you have one of those books around here, one of them witchcraft books?'

" 'I ain't got nothing around here like that; I ain't got nothing.' He got mad.

"Priest said, 'All right now, I'm going to tell you something. If you don't get it, I'll have to use it on you.'

"The man dropped his head, ran in the house, and here he come with the book. Priest looked at it and said, 'That's it, that's it. Don't you never get nothing like that. You ever get something like that again, we'll have to use it on you.'

"After that no more cattle died. That's what I've been told."[2]

Something lay heavily on George's mind. He paused and took a long breath. He seemed to drift off for a moment. Then he continued with a renewed vigor.

"I'll tell you, when I was married a few years, we were going to leave the farm down in Siberia. Dad said, 'What'd you say if we go up to Orange County. I believe there's some farms up there.'

"We went up one evening. My aunt lives up there. We stayed there overnight. And my aunt got to telling, we all got to talking about that witch business. The people living right across the field, the way I understand it, had one of these witches. And my aunt say a witch never goes across a broom.

"One day I see that woman from across the field coming there. I figure she's going to come to our house here. I went out and cut the broom. I laid it out a little away from the door. I wanted to see if there was anything to that. Finally the woman come. She was on the outside, kind of peeping in the window. She saw that broom laying there, and she hollered, 'Say hey, come out here and take this broom away from here.'

"My aunt says, 'I laid that broom for a purpose and I ain't going to take that away.'

"The woman says, 'I ain't going to cross that broom. As long as that broom laying there I ain't going in your house.'

" 'Well, then, you just have to go back home.'

"That woman went home. She wasn't going to cross that broom. My aunt, said again, 'I have heard a witch never goes across a broom.' "[3]

George's eyes lit up as his memory clicked. His words came quickly.

"Well, one time there's a fella in Siberia. He went on a train to Louisville with fifty dollars on him. And when he got home, he went over to the priest. He told the priest, 'By the way, I was riding on the train the other day, and I fell asleep, and when I woke up my fifty dollars was gone.'

" 'When was that?' the priest said.

" 'Oh, was about a month or so ago.'

"The priest said, 'Why didn't you come right away? I could have gotten that money back for you but the way it is now, I guess it's all spent, I can't do nothing about it.' "

George reflected briefly. "Now I don't know whether there's anything to it or not," he mused. Something seemed to have flashed into his mind, for he perked up and spoke strongly.

"Another thing one time out here. There's a fella over here from Germany. He told me, 'There was a man driving with his team one time.'

"I hear a lot of stuff about driving a team.

"Well, the team stopped right in its tracks. A man was driving along with the team. He got down, took them by the bridle and started pulling. They just wouldn't go, by golly.

"He looked over across the field. There's a house with two cupolas on there. He tried the harness again; they wouldn't go. Finally he got to thinking. Maybe that man has something to do with that. The driver said 'I'll tell you again, let me alone or else I'll work on you, by golly. And I'll tell you again, I ain't bothering you. Go on home.' The driver then took his horse by the bridle and yelled, 'Get up, get up!' The horses stood there, just wouldn't move.

"The driver went and got a wagon wrench from by the double tree. There's a wrench there which they take the wheels off with. He took the wrench and used it to knock one of the spokes out of the back wheels. After he done that, he looked over at the man he had just talked to a while ago. The man fell down and broke his neck. The witchcraft worked on him too."[4]

These traditional stories, related spontaneously and all on one occasion, reveal several attitudes of George. Most striking is the implied importance of maintaining peace in the community. In the first story, for instance, the "witchcraft person" asks twice, "Do you want to see the man?" George's grandfather answers no because he fears that he would hold a grudge against the culprit. In a village like Siberia, holding barely five families, maintaining harmony among neighbors was crucial to the community's existence. Yet it was often not easy. The pressure on residents to work together and the cohesion of a shared system of beliefs helped to maintain the village's social stability.[5]

The architecture and artifacts of the area reflected and reinforced the importance of living together peaceably. George points out that the witch's house had "two cupolas," a strange sight among the houses in the region. The stories support the attitude that uncommon or unconventional events or objects connote danger and engender mistrust. The common artifacts of rural life—a wagon wheel, a household broom, a wagon spoke—are used to combat witchcraft, itself a symbol for deviance from community norms.

George dramatizes his mixed feelings about witchcraft in the stories. With hindsight, George questions the reality of the witchcraft he has described. To reconcile the apparent contradiction between growing up believing in the supernatural and being an adult skeptical of such things, he develops a viewpoint that rationalizes his adult view while not betraying his childhood belief. He says, "If you don't believe in it, it can't do nothing to you. So I don't believe in that witchcraft stuff no more." With the new rationale he could offset the stigma others might attach to his childhood beliefs, while still holding on to the values he knew.[6]

Themes of power and deviance run strongly in the stories. Now that George felt out of the mainstream of life, he felt powerless. The man in one story had a book to gain power; George wondered about his presence, his power and control over his own life and that around him. It was no accident that he chose to tell so many stories on witchcraft. The stories bundled many conflicts that were occurring in his life. He grew up with one entrenched tradition, yet now he felt out of touch with the continuity of newer, "modern" traditions. There was tradition around him all right, but it was not the one with which he felt familiar or comfortable.

Let's go back for a moment to Siberia, Indiana, before World War I. George's father's general store stood on the crossroads, a center for social life. George remembered seeing men gather there to swap stories and to whittle objects such as chains and caged balls. Young George was fascinated by the dexterity these men exhibited with a pocketknife and wood. At the age of ten, he was making things like they did. "I wouldn't do without a pocketknife. I would take that knife and whittle stuff out."

George also liked to watch the village blacksmith: "I used to stand and watch him weld irons, and hammer out plow shares, and shoe horses." Early in life, George was developing an appreciation for the creative manipulation of natural materials.

George even connected his fondness for manipulating things with baseball, which was a source of great pride for a rural boy. It stressed ingenuity and physical prowess. George told me about making baseballs and bats out of scrap materials: rags tightly bound for balls and carved woods for bats. Baseball was the way boys got together with other boys from nearby villages. Inherently pastoral and socially engaging, baseball was one way boys called attention to individual skills and gained leveling social values within a community setting.

To hear George tell it, the residents of Siberia enjoyed a harmonious, structured way of life. George returned to this theme often. He recalled the value of older ways of doing things, for example, when he described his adjustment to so-called technological advances.

"Some people say, 'I want to go back to the old times,' and some people say, " 'What do you want to go back to the old times for? You'd have to get out there with the old wooden plow, plow the fields where nowadays they got tractors to get out there.'

"In a way if you go back, they had their hard times, but they also got them now, yeah. But *now's* what's bringing our heart attacks on.

"Yeah, I went through a lot of baloney—eighty years. Things altogether different then than what they are now. I just wonder where things going to go if they keep on going the way they are—the way all this killing and robbing and shooting and raping and everything's going on."

The darker side of progress has shaken Americans' faith in advanced technology. Nuclear accidents, walkway collapses, automobile recalls, and machinery defects have taken some of the shine off what some have dubbed "the age of technology," "the hi-tech revolution," or "the postmodern world of electronics." There are those who prefer the security and satisfaction of a structured, traditional life, accepting change with caution, wary of giving up traditions for the new. They try to reconcile old with new, traditional with modern, hand with machine.

Change in Huntingburg crept slower than in other places, but George felt the winds of change blowing ever more quickly. According to George's way of thinking, technological progress has had, on the whole, bad consequences. Having been brought up in a farming community, his values are agrarian, which hold that closeness to nature, work with one's hands, and reverence for the land assure qualities of wholesomeness and goodness.[7] Images may come to your mind of Mother Earth, farmers, Bohemians. But everyday people feel this uncertainty about the march of time and progress, and the place of tradition and past ways of doing things in our lives. Ever the academic, folklorist Richard Dorson back in Bloomington realized the alternative worldview when he lay perilously close to death after a heart attack brought on by the stress of deadlines and demands characteristic of the post-modern world. He thought that "folkloric behavior, frowned on by the urban middle classes, provides mortals with ego reassurances and satisfactions while avoiding the fierce stress of competitive individualism in modern life."[8]

Despite George's personal feelings of ambivalence, he functioned adequately in his job at the furniture factory and in his social relations. Nevertheless, within his new industrial surroundings at Huntingburg, he periodically felt conflicts and insecurities. To many, Huntingburg is hardly a bustling metropolis, but to George, who had come of age in tiny Siberia, the spaces were larger and haughtier, and the values were different. Where was the harmony, the love of the land, the glory of the toiling hand?

"I run a lathe when I was young, but over there at the factory, that was a *machine*. I never did like the job so finally I told the foreman, 'If anybody wants that job, I'd sooner have the job sanding.' I don't know if you ever hear about that, an ash-sander. That's turning what I sand *by hand*.

"I tell you, my dad had a store. I was about sixteen years old. And one day I noticed I was getting a little mustache, a little beard. I asked, 'Dad can I have one of them old razors.' He said, 'Here, you take this here.' Well, I used that about a year and, by golly, some way or another I heard so much about these new safety razors. Well, I got one of them. But, hell, I didn't keep it long. Shit, I didn't like the damn thing, and I gave it to my brother Matt. I went back to my old razor, and that's what I use yet, the old straight razor."

George's account reminds us that modernity, rather than always eliminating folk beliefs and practices, often reinforces them in people.[9] George's description of his shaving methods, minor in itself, points to the important mental adjustments he had to make when he moved from the traditional life of rural Siberia to industrial Huntingburg.[10]

George talks much like the old traditional men that folklorist Henry Glassie found in Ireland. Their surroundings were changing, physically and socially. Industrial progress brought comfort, they were told. One man, Hugh Nolan, spoke for others when he told Glassie that the coming of the automobile, television, and electricity in his lifetime has "brought a great improvement to the people. But the greatest change in my lifetime has been that people has lost all respect for authority, civil or divine. Today there is neither law nor order. And that is the greatest change." Eloquently he summed up the feeling stirring within. "Aye, the two things happen at the one time. Things get better. And they get worse."[11] Conflicts and uncertainties arise as surroundings and lives change. Those conflicts can stew inside, or be dramatized by the person who makes things like stories or carvings.

George originally moved to Huntingburg on the advice of his brother Matt, who said that a job would bring in more money than farming. Being experienced with woodworking, George found a job in the Huntingburg Furniture Factory, and he resettled his family in Huntingburg. His specialty was working the glue clamp. "I glued all kinds of boards. They cut them in little strips, knots and everything were taken out, and then they brought them to me, and then I had to glue them together. That's where I learned a lot of my gluing for cutting stuff out, the carving." He could adjust to industrial life because he had a job where he could use his hands and work with wood. Sharing the day with other workers from rural backgrounds also helped him feel comfortable.

Problems arose though. George developed cataracts on his eyes. George described the problem by referring to a particular experience.

"One day the foreman come in there and said, 'Say George, you're getting joints in your gluing.'

"I said, "I'm doing it like I always have and I can't see *nothing*."

" 'Come out here where it's brighter then.'

"And when I goes through the plant you *can* see them little black streaks there."

After thirty-five years at the factory, and a cataract operation, George realized that he could not work at the factory much longer. The prospect of not working at the glue clamp bothered him because of the great pride he had in his manual abilities. In his childhood, the elderly had traditionally been respected for their knowledge, but such respect was not forthcoming at the factory. A younger, hipper generation had come up to replace many of the old-timers. They ribbed the old men about their backhome ways. George told a story about a girl and a coffee cup to illustrate their attitude.

"A girl near here had kind of a little coffee cup somebody had given her as a present. She dropped it one day and broke the handle off it. She brought it by one day.

"I said, 'Say, by the way, let that over here, I can put that handle back on there for you.'

"Well, she says sassy-like, 'Well how are you going to put that back on, old-timer?'

"I said, 'Don't never mind just let that here. I'll put that on there.'

"I went in and got my glue out here, smeared it on there. About two hours later she come out here.

" 'Well, I'll be doggone!' she squealed, 'You got that handle back on. You can't even see that it's broke off!'

"And the last time I saw her was about a year later. 'Have you still got that thing with the handle on it?' I asked her.

" 'Yeah,' she said, 'I guess you know something.'

"If you had seen that handle, you'd said, 'Well, hell, you can't never get that handle back.' Yeah, I learned that gluing over there when I worked in the factory and all that stuff. Shit, I was good on that stuff."

George associated repair work of this sort with the duties his grandfather had had on the family farm in Siberia. His familiarity with the cooperative labor of those days contributed to his later resentment of the hierarchic authority at the factory. Like other older workers, George found that his seniority was a liability rather than an advantage.

"I was working on the glue clamp and it got so that they shipped in quite a bit of lumber. I didn't have regular work on the glue clamp

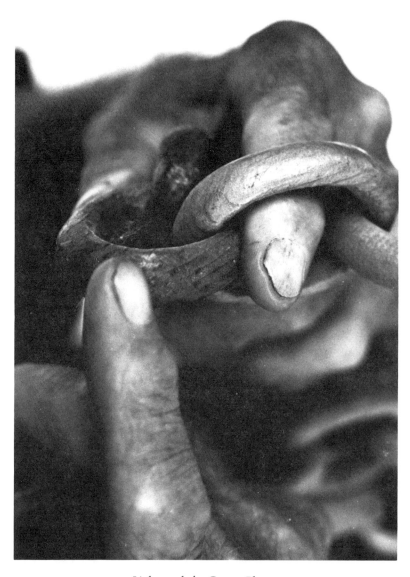

Links made by George Blume

and then they had to shove me out on this place and that place and then they shoved me back in on the glue clamp—and I didn't like that. Why, I had a high seniority you know. I was one of the oldest men that worked there.

"Another job came up and I bid on her and I got her. But I had this superintendent and he was kind of an old crabass. And he wanted me to stay on there. I said, 'Hell no, I bid on that other! I ain't going to work in there.'

'You'll be sorry of it; you'll be sorry of it!' he said.

"One evening, goddamn, they put it out, 'Now we're going to want four men to come back here and clean up after quitting time. Take about an hour. That goes for senior too. Whoever got the highest seniority, they get the job.' Well, I was one of them.

"One evening I was sweeping up the floor in there, that big machine room there. Finally, hell, this old superintendent comes through. I said, 'Oh boy, goddamn, I guess very likely I done something wrong; I'm going to get my ass eat out.'

"And I say if you get a job you don't like, can't handle it right, you better get out or it will—it will *kill* you!"

Pushed aside at work and feeling like an odd man out, George looked for something to raise his prestige in the eyes of others and in his own mind. He found it in carving. Sixty-year old George saw a wooden chain an old man had made. It evoked his childhood. Whittling held a new fascination for him.

"When I see the wooden chain the first time, I heard it took him twelve years to make that log chain. I said, 'Hell, I can make those things . . . yeah, I can do it.' Now he made it different from what I did. When he made it, that was all together. It wasn't glued or nothing.

"Well, I just got a signal one evening there. I got to thinking, 'I'm going to try to cut out something out of wood.' Well, I had a pocketknife since I went to grade school already. Whittled stuff like this here dart and whimmy-diddle. Later on, doggone, after I went to work in the factory, see how that wood was left out to grab, I got an idea. I seen about that chain. I'd make a link, I'd make another link, and another. And then I'd take that apart and then I had a chain link here, and here, and there. Then I'd glue that up, and I had three links there. And then I made three more like that. That's the way

I kept on making it till I had about fifteen or sixteen links. That's
the way I kept on going. . . .

"When after I seen that I could do it, I got real interested. I liked
them chains, by golly. Hell, I had them down to even watch chains—
little, little. Now if somebody else made it for me, I wouldn't have
got the kick out of it. But yeah, I made that see. . . . *I* made that. I
made eight or ten of those things I bet. I got kick out of it, just natural-
ly making things."

George didn't make the chain as other carvers did. Usually, the
carver brags about not using glue, screws, or splits to hold the links.
But George used his skills of gluing, sanding, and shaping. He compensated for the violation by making extra-special chains—replicas
of long log chains or remarkably small watch chains. The objects
stirred him. He had found something that made him feel creative and
alleviated his tensions. George explained his newly found self-worth
by describing what happened when he brought the chains to work.

"A lot of people say, '*Well how in the hell do you put them
together?*' I mean you can't see that glue. I used to be so damn good
on that gluing. Like them log chains. I learned that gluing over there
when I worked in the furniture factory.

"A few days after I made that chain, I come over there to the factory. There's a bunch of them boys sitting over there on Fourth Street.
They looked at it and said, 'Hey, I didn't know you made stuff like
that! I would have come and seen some of that if I had known.'

"Yeah, when I made that first chain, I took that over to the store
one evening. A man come in there and said, 'Say, you really done a
wonderful job on that thing. Goddamn, that's really . . . that's good
workmanship on there.' "

George used his whittling skills learned in childhood and his gluing skills learned at the factory to make an evocative symbol of his
identity. He made his presence known through creativity, because
he could display it to others and to himself. It also helped him cope
with changes that threatened him. When he chose words for his story,
he underscored his "job" and "work"—troublesome areas for him.
That, together with encouragement by viewers of his chains egged
him on to make more.

George's half chamber pot, pliers, and chamber pot

By around 1958, when he took up carving again, George's children had grown and left home, and he faced mounting friction with his wife. Her diabetic condition and frequent complaints compounded his problems at home. He responded by putting a workshop in his basement, where, in the evenings, he carved chains, caged balls, pliers, locks, and small figures out of scrap wood from the factory. Like others before and after him, George countered unacceptable emotional impulses with creative energy. The renowned American painter Thomas Hart Benton, to give one example, said of his creative period in Chicago: "By the time I went to Chicago there were moments when my uneasiness was intolerable. As the spells came on, the desire to submerge myself in the loneliness of strange places and peoples bit me like a hot flame. The intimacies of the military school burned me up, and though I controlled my inner rages there, sitting alone secretively chewing tobacco, I dived into Chicago as into a cool bath. Every artist in a world of "practical" men shares somewhat the uneasiness I describe, but those who came out of the Middle West at the beginning of the century, I imagine, have had a larger dose than all others."[12]

Benton's scorn for the aesthetic sensibilities of the Midwest aside, others have sought solace through creativity because of the way it can block out tension or give one a feeling of starting over. Richard Dorson, a writer whose productivity awed his colleagues, attributed his drive that produced his largest work to an abortive romance and feelings of rootlessness.[13] Michael Owen Jones noticed that a Kentucky chairmaker built unusual chairs with an imposing sense of enclosure when he felt threatened. Jones concluded that grieving and creating are closely connected. "In grief there is loss, followed by a feeling that the world is empty and poor; in communicating through expressive structures such as stories and songs there is filling the void caused by the loss, first a state of doubt and then order and belief and wholeness once more."[14] Whether a person is a folk or elite artist has little to do with it. Jones made sure to state that there are happy poets and artists, but he pointed to bereavement as one strong motive for creativity. "The individual who has suffered loss is charged with nervous energy, sensitive to the human condition, and most aware of himself and his own frailty," Jones wrote. Years before Jones made his comment, Sigmund Freud noted how people look to creative work for displacement of unacceptable instincts. He failed to explain the displacement mechanism in detail, but he did understand that satisfactions from "an artist's joy in creating, in giving his phantasies body" had a "special quality" which was "finer and higher."[15] George Blume personified this rationale.

The unusual object he brought to the factory drew attention and prestige to its maker. George boasted that he had made the chain "by himself," and that made him feel self-reliant. He gained a sense of accomplishment from taking on a challenge and meeting it in what he considered a unique way—the use of glue. With the chain completed in a week or so, as opposed to the twelve years it took to make the chain he saw in 1958, it was as if he had reshaped and transformed himself. He felt different, even though his life itself had not changed. The cutting and gluing became a ritual of transformation, and he controlled the ritual.

Major changes were to come, however. Shortly after his wife died in 1959, George retired. Faced with sudden loneliness, he again carved to reduce his anxieties. "If you sit there and don't do nothing," George asserted, "you go to thinking about that bad stuff. There's a lot of things that'll drive you nuts. When I started to whittle out

George's carving of Grandpa hauling produce

them things, by gosh, I put my mind *all* on there. *That'd take the worrying away from me, you see.* Yeah, after she died, I was by myself." He sighed. Looking back, he realized that carving helped him keep his balance. He put his mind on his carving and he drew on the control and escape it provided. Then he "got into his mind" to carve other objects besides chains.

George compulsively carved buildings and activities he remembered from childhood. He made old tools, plows, threshers. He had log buildings, wooden shoes, churches, and scenes of quilting bees and harvests. "I made old-timers," he emphasized, "I don't care for the new stuff." Many carvings had a figure of his grandfather—an important role model. A log cabin was a backdrop for his grandfather standing with captured game and homey chairs. Another carving showed him driving a team of horses. George also made humorous pieces. As a parody of technology, he made an "electric ass wiper," a corncob attached to an electric cord. Another humorous piece was a chamber pot sliced in half with the inscription "for my half-assed friends."

Rarely did he show his pieces to others. He did give away chains to some of his children and he occasionally displayed the chains to others, but his other pieces were part of a private world he created in his basement. Making the buildings and figures became addictive, increasingly occupying his time and injecting into his life escape and euphoria. Eventually he completed almost a thousand pieces.

"When I asked him about the sources for his ideas, he replied, just a matter of sitting there thinking about the old place, old ways, good ways—Grandpa sitting there playing the fiddle, two deer hanging up there—so I made that thing." Faced with a difficult adjustment to retirement and loneliness, he looked to, and materialized, memories of childhood. He considered that time simpler and easier. Carving had been part of his turning from a boy to a man. With his childhood use of tools and knowledge of woods, he was ready for the tasks lying ahead as a working adult. In middle age he had work, family, and friends occupying his time and mind. Nearing retirement, being alone, he used carving to help adjust to a new stage of life, as it had helped him adjust earlier in life.

In old age, George adjusted to his alienation from the mainstream, youthful society—a society marked by modern technological values. He told a story to illustrate the difference between traditional values and modern ones.

"A lady come to me one time. She seen that Ferris wheel I made. She says, 'Where do you attach that electric end to run that thing?'

"And I said, 'Hell, there ain't no electric on there. That's run by sand.'

" 'By sand? I want to see that. Start it up once!'

"Well, it went around and around.

" 'Doggone,' she says, 'I thought that thing was run by electric.'

" 'But it's run by sand. See that's the way they used to do it!'

"They run them mills you know, them flour mills, that way. They run by water, water going over the mill. That's where I got the idea of running sand over the mill. But these people forget that."

When George explicitly says "these people forget that," he implicitly says "these people are forgetting me, for that knowledge is my knowledge." George's carvings and his behavior toward them are reactions, in many ways, to a conflict between the rural way of life he absorbed as a child and the rise of industrial modernity around him. His carvings do more than get his mind off his troubles. They also reinforce, to himself and to others that his old beliefs and skills matter. The repetition of the wood-carving skills and forms provides continuity, and therefore importance.

Not surprisingly, symbols of death occur in George's carving. His wife died. Many friends died. He once shared a hospital room with a boyhood friend who was dying. He remembered, too, his son's graphic accounts of the slaughter of the Korean War. Death seems closer in winter, in the darkness and cold. The frigid air takes away George's breath. The ice and snow take away his balance. His heart races at every chill, and his head aches from every gust. He sits inside his stark room often feeling trapped by the elements. Spring means freedom; spring brings renewal. But first he has to arm-wrestle against winter's grip. So I didn't find presents or the approaching new year occupying his mind when I saw him at Christmas. I heard about death.

"A lot of people, they go to shovel snow; they die and fall over dead. It's mostly old people that sit in the house, don't do nothing— and here comes that snow. That works on their heart. That kills them. Yeah, I said, pal, I'm eighty-one years old, and I went through a lot of that crap.

"Lot of people ask me how I'm making it. I tell them I'm making it all right. If I don't get no worse, I might never die."

Among his carvings was a hearse and coffin. "In Siberia," George smiled, "they carried you away in the same wagon they hauled the manure in, and that's what I made there." He made other reminders of death. "I made my own keys to heaven. When I wants to get to heaven," he explained, "I won't ask Saint Peter. I'll just unlock it myself." He had made an electric chair. "That's a terrible way to go, and I seen it in the paper, so I made it." It turned out that his sister Minnie had died from an accidental electrocution. He made gallows and gravestones. Rather than denying death, he toyed with it. His carvings of death appeared on the surface to be strange, whimsical, funny, and playful. But the extra coat of play he applied to the grim objects affirmed that the issue beneath was more disturbing. Like humor and play, which have the function of indirectly broaching sensitive topics, George's objects became symbols of his inner sensitivities.

What other internal feelings had been brought out through the

George with his German barn

control and expression of carving? George's failing eyesight and hearing, coupled with fears of alienation and death, made him feel confined. A carving of a man attached to a ball and chain dramatized his feeling.

"There's a man I made there with a twelve-foot chain, made out of wood, and that was buckled around his legs and locked there. And on the end of that chain, there's a big ball, and that was supposed to be iron. And that iron weighed just heavy enough so that man could pick that thing and walk away with it. But he couldn't run with it. That was made so you couldn't run away, you know. And then, in the evening, they put them men in their cells. That's the way I felt sometimes."

George indeed couldn't run away, but his carvings gave him escape. His chains became favored tools of escape because they also symbolized prevalent themes on his mind: tradition, death, and confinement.

In 1972, George was struck by an automobile and almost killed. His daughter, who also lives in Huntingburg, offered to take him into her home. To pay for his care, she sold his carvings. He could part with them because they reminded him of his frailty and frustration. He tried making a few chains after he moved, but he could not see the lines he drew in the wood. He could not hold his knife steady. A man has a special relationship to his tools, and when George lost control of his cutting tools, his carved world slipped away.

He made up for the loss of his carving by gardening more, with an aesthetic sensibility. Why do I say that? George expressed himself through the things he made, and grew, and he wanted to tell me how he felt about the friendship we had struck up. He couldn't give me a chain as a friendship token as he would have liked, so he gave me the natural beauty of a Chinese lantern plant with its delicate orange-red seed cases. "Yeah I grew that myself. Not many can do them like that you know." He still had the creative spirit.

So mornings he would be out gardening around town, still insisting on using a hand-powered mower. He trudges slowly from place to place. Cars and children race by him. His feet flounder occasionally, but he walks proudly, for every step is an achievement of keeping balance. Walking by himself is independence. Others can see that he is alive indeed, and out of a nursing home. Although he doesn't need

it, he keeps a post-office box. Maybe he does need it, for it is something
he can call his, and it beckons him to town. What used to take a few
minutes now takes the better part of an hour or more, but he is proud
of the self-powered steps that take him. Going to the post office gives
his day some structure and direction.

George sometimes stops at the home of a widow whom he fan-
cies. He tends to her garden. She makes him tea. She laughs at his
stories. He shows concern for her complaints. She listens to his com-
mentaries on the state of the world. They comfort each other. They
talk about the deep troubles they feel, and the wondrous joys they
find in nature, in making things, in waking up to another spring day.
It's time to return home. Isn't it funny, he thinks, how they
sometimes feel like children coming home from play, how they now
answer to their own children, but how their rushing children can't
appreciate the small acheivements of living, and the depth and detail
of life they can sense at their snail's pace?

I have an especially vivid memory of George from the summer
of 1980. He sat on his porch in his familiar farmer's overalls and he
told me that he was, "yeah, winding down all right." He said he was
prepared for death. He tried to make a joke. "They had it in the paper
that our pope, he kicked the bucket. They dies just like we do, yeah."
He grinned weakly and turned to look, as best he could, into the
distance. I showed him a few of his carvings that I had been able to
obtain. His face glowed. He held them in his large, quavering hands.
"Well I'll be doggone," he drawled. "You hang on to them things,
by God, you hear, like I hung on, yeah. I went through a lot of crap
you know. So you *hang on* to them things!" His hands eased carefully over the texture he made years earlier, almost as if he was checking that his creative imprint, his experience and effort, still remained.
Satisfied, he placed the carvings in my hands. "Thanks," he said.
"Hang on to that."

FLOYD'S STORY

Wrestling Boys, Schools, and Escapes

Although not the storyteller that George is, Floyd Bennington
referred to his past often in our conversations. After I had known him
for almost three years, I sat in his living room and he handed me
photos from his Plainville, Indiana, youth. The old photos came out

of a modern cabinet. This was his life, the old covered over by the new. I looked around at his modern furniture, and I recalled the chair he was really proud of, down in his basement. He had made it.

I returned to his photos: the log house in which he had grown up; Grandpa's birthday party, with cake after cake lining the long farm table out-doors; the one-room schoolhouse where he taught. Floyd cherished this photograph of boys and girls sitting rigidly around a pot-bellied stove while he stood in front of a wall on which hung a flag, a chart of the human anatomy, and letters in the best penmanship. As these photos brought out his memories, his wife would fill in details of names and dates. I took the opportunity to ask him, "What do you consider the significant experiences in your life?" He quietly answered, "I'll have to think about that." A few days later I received this account:

"I, Floyd Eli Bennington, was born on a cold damp morning in the fall of 1902, September 27, in a small four-room farm home, two miles west of Plainville in Steele Township, Daviess County, Indiana. Dad called Dr. Reeve from Edwardsport, Indiana, a town about six miles from where we lived. He arrived in a short time in his horse-drawn buggy. After the great event was over, Dad said "Doc, how much do I owe you?" Doc answered, "I guess five dollars will do. He isn't very big—just five pounds."

"On my arrival, I was welcomed by a six-and-a-half-year-old brother, Virgil. In about two and one-half years another brother, John, arrived. He and I, being nearly the same age, shared our play things and games. When I grew older I could help dad with the farm work. I helped by feeding the stock and chickens and milking the cows. I helped mother a lot with her work. John and I played several games with the neighbor kids, the change of seasons bringing different games.

"Christmas was a highlight in everyone's life. Dad was just the right size and shape to make a good Santa Claus. He would dress in his red suit and beard, and come to our house, then go to three or four other places. We each hung our stockings on chairs in front of the fireplace for Santa to fill. An orange, some peanuts and candy, usually some stick candy, a cap buster and firecrackers were almost a routine course and perhaps small objects like a pocketknife, a pair of gloves, a harmonica, skates—but very few toys and games. I was

Floyd Bennington's family, Plainville, Indiana, ca. 1900

about twelve years old before I knew that Santa couldn't get down the chimney. I came home from school one day and went nosing around and found the articles which I was to get. That was the bluest Christmas I ever had. Roast goose and all the trimmings was our regular dinner for the Christmas day. We raised our own geese on the farm.

"During the school season it was our pleasure to go to one-room school, all eight grades. Here we played baseball, wrestled, jumped, played marbles, shinny—a forerunner of the game of hockey. We used a tiny can for a puck and clubs were cut from the fence row. In the cold winter we did ice skating and we used a sponge rubber ball for a puck instead of the tin can. There was a few dunkings by some of the daredevils skating on a spot of too thin ice. Many games of running, pulling, hiding, daring that required physical strength were our favorites.

"When out of school there was rabbit hunting, fishing, trapping, sleigh riding. Of course there were some farm jobs that had to be done. There were fences to build and repair, firewood to cut, corn to shuck, hay to harvest. Sometimes it was put in the farm hay loft; other times it was stacked in the field. Weeds had to be cut from the garden and truck patches. Wild berries were picked in the summer. My mother made them into delicious berry pies. There was one form of fishing that we enjoyed in the summertime. We would get into the creek and wade along until we found a sunken hollow log. We would bank it and dump out the catfish that were in it. When the old river beds or bayous would dry up in the summer we would catch the fish with pitchforks.

"Dad cut our own hair and when I reached the age of twelve he trained me how to do the job. During the summer there were ten or twelve boys who would gather in our pasture to play baseball. They would take turns playing and coming in for me to cut their hair. I got short changed in the ball playing.

"After the circus had been in town, we would try a few acrobatics in the barn loft. Our games were usually imitations of the activities in season. Basketball was just beginning in southern Indiana the last two or three years that I was in grade school. We didn't have much sophisticated equipment. We used a tomato basket nailed on the end of the barn for a goal.

"In the river bottom land was our home at this time. The old creek was kind of tricky. Some places it was wide and shallow, other places it might be eight-foot or ten-foot deep. One such place we called the 'old swimming hole.' We cut a good sized pole and anchored it under a root of a tree on the bank. This we used for our diving board. We enjoyed many pleasant hours there. It also served as our bathtub. Here in this portion of the West Fork of the White River in Steele Township, the river overflowed. In 1913 there was one of the greatest floods that anyone at that time could remember. It rained, rained and more rain until the water began to surround our house. Dad brought the boat up to the back door to the kitchen and tied it to the door knob. Several times during the night he was up checking on it. Just about daybreak the water started coming into our house. He and Virgil brought large blocks in and placed most of the furniture on them. As soon as we had our breakfast, we started making preparations to move out and go to Uncle Tom's place which was on higher ground, on a small knoll. Everything loaded and ready, when we arrived at our fence along the east side we found it had washed down and across the lane. We had to reverse the course and go across our pasture. We loaded into the wagon with high side boards on it. We had two calves, twenty pigs in the bed, and two cows strung behind. Mom, Virgil, John, and me in the wagon caused the mule to go off into deep water, splashing over the mule's back. The mule's foot was caught in the wire fence of our pasture. God sent a miracle and unfastened the mule's foot and we went safely over. The water got eighteen inches deep in our house and it was a week before we could return home.

"In the fall of 1917 I started Plainville High School. I drove a horse and buggy, horseback or a bicycle to school. The first day of school I was accepted as a green country farm boy. One of the elite town boys, who was almost a head taller than I, was going to make me prove myself. He kept punching, pushing, and shoving me around until we finally clenched in a wrestling match. He hadn't been pitching hay, shocking wheat or doing all the hard muscle jobs as a farm boy does. So I did not have much trouble pinning him down three times. That was the last of that and we were good friends ever after.

"The first year of high school I didn't have much too much trouble. I took manual training for one subject. It was all woodwork, no machines but a wood lathe. I enjoyed it immensely and it was a two period class, ninety minutes, but there was no preparation or book work to do.

"World War I was drawing a little closer to Armistice Day, November 11, 1918. The summer was similar to most summers except many things were rationed and in short supply. I started my sophomore year and after a few weeks we had some peas on the farm that had to be taken care of. Help was very scarce so high school boys were permitted to miss school to help with the farm crops. I had to help with the hay. I missed most of the baseball games but did get to play basketball. I had another course in manual training this year.

"Country schools had pie suppers and box socials and plays to raise money for necessary school items. Late in October one of these rural schools was having a social of the sort. I got up enough nerve to ask a pretty little blue-eyed, brown-haired girl if I could take her to the pie supper. Delpha was her name. She accepted and we went to this even on our first date.

"When World War I was over I had moved from my birthplace home to my mother's father's home on the sand farms in a different area of Steele Township. Dad was having a very difficult time making ends meet and I had decided to go to college and be a schoolteacher. When the time came Dad did manage to accumulate sixty-five dollars and paid me for my horse. I used this and borrowed some to finish my first twelve weeks at Indiana State Normal School at Terre Haute as it was known then. I passed a test for the teacher's license and started teaching that fall at the age of eighteen. Delpha, my little blue-eyed girl, waited for me.

"I taught a rural one-room school in 1921 and 22. I did some handyman work for awhile and helped Dad with the dairy farming too. I planned to go back to college during the summer for twelve weeks.

"My sweetheart and I decided on the old adage that two can live as cheap as one, so on June 17, 1922, we were wed. We left for Terre Haute the following day. It was a lovely honeymoon. We visited Delpha's aunt in West Terre Haute.

"I continued teaching and going back to school in the summer, working odd jobs or anything I could find to do. A beginning teacher made $800 per year. I taught three rural one-room schools. Around that time the township consolidated and the remainder of my teaching was in larger schools. When I was not in school I did painting and repair work and built a few new houses for other people. I retired in 1969 with forty-seven and one-half years teaching."

"A country farm boy," Floyd writes. Floyd's rich memories of his childhood farm home, his farm chores, and the rural schools in which he taught show his close emotional ties with the rural life, even after more than thirty years in industrial communities. He describes, like many country people, the beauty and beastliness of nature. The flood reminded Floyd of his people's dependence on nature. They survive with God's help, he says, but he is awed by the power of nature.

Floyd's rural identity especially strengthens when he, a "green country farm boy" fights "one of the elite town boys." Here is the ultimate masculine test: the newcomer tagged as different proving himself in a ritual challenge of strength. Floyd pinned the town boy because, he thinks, his training camp in the country gave him the upper hand. "Prove himself." That phrase would also pop up when Floyd talked about an especially challenging carving project. Carving and wrestling do have something in common; they are both ritualistic tests of manly ability. In one, the opponent is another boy and your fear; in the other, the opponent is the wood and your impatience. Floyd's carving fits into his story, too, because it symbolizes to him his rural way of life. When he carves, he recalls the self-sufficiency of his family farm, his father's crackerjack work with wood, and boys' ingenuity with simple tools and supplies.

Floyd Bennington in his workshop

Another interview produced further connections between his present carving and past way of life.

"I didn't really start carving until 1959. I'd be shot by the day's work and I needed something to relax. I picked up whittling. I did some woodworking as a kid—I always was handy with a pocket knife, a saw and a hammer. Dad was handy with wood, too. When it came to butchering time, we always had lard to render, and we needed a paddle to stir that lard so I helped him make lard paddles. Dad always made his own double-trees, neck yokes, tongs, and things of that sort. There was also one man that lived not too far from us. He whittled a few things. And then I have seen others work with a pocketknife and make a little basket or cage like out of a peach seed, and maybe carve a little ball or monkey in it."

Floyd returned to the theme of his childhood whittling often. In other conversations he remarked that his father carved ax-handles and, in imitation, Floyd made baseball bats. Upon becoming an adult, Floyd chose an occupation that required using manual skills he had learned from his father. Floyd emphasized the handwork of his father—his role model—and the items Floyd made for his childhood games and farm work. Late in life, Floyd used carving to reinforce his belief in the intrinsic, wholesome value of handwork. "Machinery ruined us," he explained. "No one does much work by hand anymore." Like George Blume, Floyd Bennington often felt that the industrial surroundings in which he found himself often conflicted with his esteem for closeness to nature and reliance on one's hands.

Could he maintain his traditional beliefs and customs with the changes that time brings to everyone? A prominent memory that came to his mind when he reminisced was Christmas, the traditional season. The "bluest" Christmas was the one that shattered his steadfast belief in the magic of Santa Claus. Despite this early disappointment, Floyd implies that his rural background offered him a stable structure of values, a steady rock to prevent him from blowing aimlessly. He knew where he belonged and why.

Yet, he taught industrial arts. I asked him about that. When he began, manual skill was required. As machinery came in, he wanted to master it. To be able to control machinery would preserve his dominance of tools and materials and, more important, allow his hand

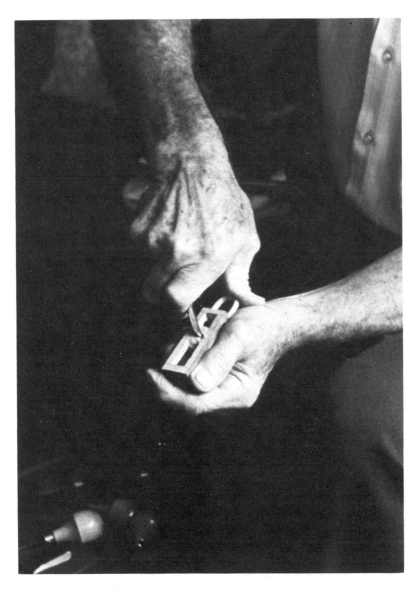

Floyd making his lantern ball-in-cage

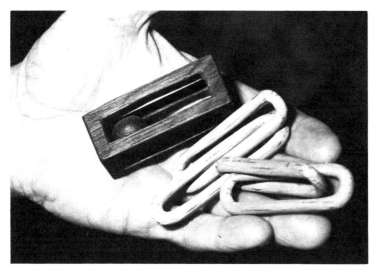

Floyd's chain and caged ball

and mind to continue to assert themselves. Teaching industrial arts was his announcement of his harnessing of the machinery. So he was able to preserve a place for his manual skills.

Floyd's account ends with his retirement in 1969. The emotional and physical problems he and his wife suffered after that came out only in other interviews. Delpha described to me Floyd's depression when he retired. "I couldn't see how he could whittle, being so nervous after he quit teaching, but he told me it was relaxing," Delpha remarked. Whittling and furniture repair work allowed him to stay active and productive in his later years, and he had something from the heart to give members of his cherished family and those he cared for. Floyd also had to escape from physical illnesses.

After retirement, he developed cancer of the prostate, and his wife's debilitating stroke and his daughter's heart disease prevented him from roaming far. He turned to carving as a form of creative escape. Carving cut at his fears and feelings of restriction.

"The reason I took whittling up in the first place is—we, by Delpha being in the condition that she was—we didn't go every place like a lot of people do. We didn't attend all of the events around. I needed something to get my mind off.

"Well, I could sit down at carving and you got to think about carving and nothing else, not your troubles, or else you might cut your finger off, so that was good exercise for me.

"My wife learned to do a little casting with a rod, and the girl did, too, so that wasn't very hard, then, for me to get out to go fishing once in a while. But then, you couldn't fish the whole season round. So, I first picked up on trying to do a little bit of carving. I had to have something that would loosen up that tension that would build up in there."

Floyd saw pictures in mechanical magazines of chains and caged balls that reminded him of chain carving in his youth. Two long carved chains hanging over the fireplace of the Reverend Ken Scherry, who lived just a few blocks up from his house also encouraged him. "I can still do that, I bet," he thought. When he completed the first chains, the compliments of friends urged him on.

He made not long chains but small and delicate ones. He spent hours sanding down the wood to a silky finish. His caged balls are perfect spheres. He sought to create an impression of perfection in his objects, of perfect working order, such as we, and he, would like in our lives but which we seldom attain.

It is Christmas 1979. Floyd is beaming, for the whole clan is visiting the house. He excuses himself and takes me down to the cellar. There, amid scattered chairs and pictures, he talks about the backlog of woodworking projects he has. "I need woodcarving now for when me and the wife don't get along," he says quietly. His carving allows him a mental escape, and a physical, for his workshop is separated from the house. Delpha and Floyd are a warm and happy couple, and his carving helps him preserve what they have. Floyd reminds me that every couple is composed of individuals. "Each link is different, see, but it's still connected." "You mean a chain?" I innocently ask. "I mean life."

Floyd puts his hand on a chain he has made. His carving is a celebration of his raising and a reaction to retirement and problems in his life. "Does carving give you a release from your problems," I ask. "That's what I do it for!" he exclaimed. "I can go to my workshop for a couple hours and be to myself." Carving fits his idea of his proper personal and social identity. It is more than activity; it is self-expression. It expresses beauty and feeling, and it speaks of his value and experience. "Part of you is in a carving, see. . . . "

WANDLEY'S STORY

Covered Wagons, Old-Timers, and Do-Nothings

"My first trip to Indiana I come in a covered wagon." Wandley Burch let the words hang in the air, making it known that his life flowed from that experience. Wandley was born in Kansas, Illinois, where his parents had come to work in the fall harvest. Their home the rest of the year was in Solsberry, Greene County, Indiana. Wandley's father was something of a jack-of-all-trades, who also ran a blacksmith shop and could make the best wagon wheels in town. Wandley was close to the family. Drafted into service for World War II, he left the farm for the Pacific.

"I guess I'm just an old country boy, an old country bumpkin." He turned to his wife and said,, "Yeah, she's a hillbilly—like me." His voice lacked defensiveness; he applied the term with a smile and love. "What about those old tools, Wandley?" I asked. "Well, you know old country boys never throw anything out. Those tools are from the good old days."

I stepped outside. I saw a modern hospital dwarfing Wandley's small frame house. Construction encroached on his drive. Across the tracks, Indiana University sprawled over the landscape. Wandley worked in those buildings. He had maintained his old horse sense even as those around him rushed for the library. Looking back on the particular brand of education he had had, he remembered valuable lessons. "That's a broad axe. You know how that works? Probably not, eh? A man can be lost in the woods and still do all right with one of these. Now here's something, that old draw knife, make shingles with it. This little tool that looks like it, that's a spoke shaver for rounding wagon spokes."

Surrounded by construction, growth, modernity, his house held reminders of the older ways of doing things. Tools, old books, scrap wood, and furniture were packed down in his basement. He explained, "Well, someone's got to pass this stuff on or else it will be forgotten." His father had passed many of the things on to Wandley. He had saved his father's anvil, placing it in his workshop for inspiration. Wandley showed it to me, and he remembered another valuable lesson: "You know there is virtue in making something yourself." He continued, "Back then on the farm, why they didn't have very much plastic and then if you wanted anything. . . . " He paused. "Why

Wandley Burch's father's blacksmith shop, ca. 1910

we never got any toys or anything. If you wanted anything you had to make it, work for it. My father encouraged us you know. Of course that might have been the way he learned." Wandley had watched his father make his tools and farm implements. Wandley's uncles had taught him to rely on his hands to supply his needs. Uncle Otto Livingston charmed the boy by carving pliers and chains out of a single block of wood. "What skill!" he thought. "How did he do that?"

Other experiences in Wandley's childhood further impressed him with a fascination of carved objects. He told me, "A lot of the old timers, you know, used to just set around and whittle in these country stores. Even in wintertime, around my home my dad and my brothers whittled out—generally it was a little wooden wagon. They generally of a winter night they'd get in the house and start whittling. I mean working at it." Whittling was working, and carving skills were important on the farm. "I worked with wood just about the most thing we had to work with, and you had to know to use them tools." But whittling also brought into play an aesthetic sense.

Wandley continued to outline his life. In 1941, Wandley was in the army, an officer's driver. As in any war, there are moments be-

Wandley's chain, with family pictures, in his kitchen

Wandley's links with swivel and weights

tween fighting of silence and boredom. Wandley knew those troubled idle times well. Some of his buddies sat and waited for the next
move. Wandley carved. "What else should an old country boy do when
he's bored?" Using his hands, concentrating on his knife and wood,
relaxed him and occupied him.

    After the war, Wandley returned to the family farm. He married
and raised two children. Farming is not an easy or lucrative life, even
if it gives, as Wandley insists, moral rewards. To supplement his in-
come, Wandley took on carpentry jobs. Less than twenty miles away,
new limestone buildings took up the place of farms. Indiana University grew rapidly during the 1960s. Wandley joined the call for workers
and moved to Bloomington in 1967. In this busy university town,
Wandley and his fellow workers continued to whittle on their breaks
from work. After a day of putting in steps and boards, to go home
and work on small, crafty chains was delight. "These were good
carpenters, older men," Wandley pointed out. He knew respect for
the wisdom of the old from his farm days. Wandley would sit with
the older men and pull out his pocketknife, working over a block of
wood. A pair of pliers from the single block took a few minutes, so
it became the standard thing to make.

Around 1973, Wandley developed high blood pressure, which forced him to retire in 1974. In retirement, Wandley took on longer projects such as chains, caged balls, and a crown of thorns—an interlocking series of wooden sticks that formed a crown. He said of his carving, "Yeah, it settled my nerves." It helped too, he felt, for his health improved after a few years.

After finishing a number of carvings, he often set them up on his porch. He might sell one or two, but he would use the occasion to talk, "to visit" with acquaintances. He also gave wooden chains to his friends and family as tokens of friendship. Thus, he used carving partly to compensate for the loneliness that the loss of his workaday world brought. "People don't visit in town you know; they always did in the country," he said. His carvings enhanced his social ties; they gave him an introduction to friend and stranger alike.

Wandley's carvings also dealt with the changes around him that made his "country boy" identity feel odd. He carved objects remembered from his youth. He had a wooden axe stuck into a small log, a butter churn that opens its top to reveal its center, a small farmhouse whose roof lifts off, and a husking peg that once made his youthful palms sore but that now gave him nostalgic memories.

Wandley also made things that commented on the advance of machinery. He showed a "bullshit grinder," a square gadget with a crank on top. The gadget parodied the lure of cranks, buttons, and knobs on machinery, and as Wandley wryly told some guests, "It's quite an instrument, a b.s. grinder. *It's a do-nothing!* It's kind of like living any more; you don't get any place." In Wandley's laughter, however, could be heard his feelings about retirement.

Wandley also touched on confinement and restriction when he talked about chain carving. I asked him to tell me when he decided to make chains rather than cages. He replied, "When I feel chained, I make chains; when I feel caged, I make cages." Although he originally revived carving to compensate for his debility, he later carved more in reaction to his retirement. Besides coping with sudden idleness and the loss of the social life of the workaday world, he had to adjust to the additional time with his wife, Ruby. Carving in his basement gave him purpose, while she pursued her day's activities upstairs. "Yeah, the boss get onto me if I get to aggravating her and I goes off and whittles," he once offhandedly remarked. Sometimes he looked to the basement just for time to recollect himself.

Wandley with his B.S. grinder

Carving provided a welcome distraction from the stress in 1979 of caring for Ruby's father, who was slowly dying. Wandley and Ruby had moved to father's farm to care for him. To help solve his grief, Wandley would go off to a nearby stream, immerse himself in nature, and whittle. Also, at this time, Wandley's brother unexpectedly died. When I visited Wandley after this period, Wandley showed me a two-foot caged ball and a three-foot chain—his largest carvings to date—as if to imply that a connection did exist between what was on his mind and what came from his pocketknife.

Wandley continued to walk down his avenue with the help of his handmade canes. He would stop if he sees someone he knows. "What have you got there?" his acquaintance asks. "Well take a look. Bet you don't know how I made it!" When his acquaintance views and touches the chain, Wandley has reached him. Wandley came to Indiana in a covered wagon, and, now, the skills he learnt long ago give significance to his old age. Secretly proud, yet playing down the importance of his carvings, Wandley says "Go ahead, stick it in your pocket if you like it."

EARNEST'S STORY

Woods, Dogs, and Boys

I stood in Earnest's bedroom and admired the woodcarvings on a table near his bed. Earnest reached over and picked out one particular carving. "A few years ago," he said, "I was going through my father's things and found this." He held up a wooden chain attached to a caged ball that he had made as a twelve-year-old boy in Fairplay, Kentucky. "I guess I started whittling when I was three years old. My father was hired to take some men for witnesses for a trial twenty-eight miles away in a two-horse surrey. Dad was gone several days and when he came home he brought me a knife. I suppose I started cutting everything out including my fingers."

Earnest grew up in Kentucky hill country in southern Adair County. Fairplay is known to its residents but to few mapmakers. "Near Simpson Ridge," Earnest says, but he realizes that doesn't help much either. "Glensfork?" "I think that's on the map," I tell him. The places he knew as a child may not be on the map, but the feelings and knowledge he gained of growing up in a tightly knit community would always be with him. The country around Fairplay was rich in

Earnest Bennett with the chain and caged ball he made when he was twelve

timber and game. His father worked for a lumber company which "cut virgin timber for logs and staves."

Earnest was born in 1905. Young Earnest marvelled at the woods around him and his father's work with wood. As he felt the surface of the chain, Earnest recalled, "Dad hauled timber by wagon over dirt roads, mud when it rained. The lumber was in the form of saw logs, barrel staves, and turned column posts—those pretty turned posts were used to hold up the roof over front porches all over the country."

Around 1910, Earnest's father moved the family a few miles from Fairplay to a sixty-acre farm. Earnest described the farm as "ten acres of woods, five springs, a good-size creek running through, a big orchard of several kinds of apples, pears, and peaches, and a picturesque old log cabin in the back of the farm near a good spring." Earnest boasted of the handwork men in the area did with woods. "There was plenty of wood for rails, pickets for fences, tobacco sticks, and clapboards. We worked all these things up with crosscut saws, axes, maul wedges, and gluts—not chain saws then." For Earnest, chainsaws are not in the category of true tools, which, strictly speaking, are powered by men. Chainsaws answer to a motor and gasoline. Working with wood was manual. It was working with nature, rather than against it.

Imitating his elders, young Earnest worked with his pocketknife. He developed his manual dexterity, his tool sense, and his respect for the woods around him. He made wooden guns, whistles, and other toys out of the "daily supply of wood for heating the house and cooking the food." He also delighted in carving imitations of implements found on the farm. "My brother and I made a good-size wheel wagon. It looked very much like Dad's big-road wagon." Trying to explain his motives Earnest said, "I guess it was to have things to play with. My only bought toy, aside from my knife, was a ten-cent cap pistol. At about age eight or ten, when I would see a new toy or a thing I wanted, I would go home and make one for myself." Play involves wonder and fantasy but also learning. It teaches the young moral and social values. Earnest learned to imitate the skills and forms of the adult world through carving, and he indulged in being a child, too, through carving.

A man with the unusual name of Bacon Godberry got Earnest started on chain carving. Godberry was an old man, a neighbor, with a joker's personality. He showed the chain to the boy and dared him to figure out the puzzle. Figuring it became as important as making it. A boy's mind rises to such a challenge, Earnest felt, because it tests mechanical skills, problem-solving, and craftiness. Once he had it figured out, Earnest showed the chain to friends. They recognized the chain as a trophy, for it embodied symbols of prestige—woodworking and adaptability—prized in the community.

After Earnest's father built a blacksmith shop around 1917, Earnest often sat in the shop and carved while his father shaped items at the forge. Earnest looked to his father's creativity in iron for ideas. He made an analogy between his crafting new forms out of natural materials and his father's work in iron. At the shop, Earnest saw the social value of whittling, too. He remembered that his father whittled "shavings" and toys while chatting with friends during idle moments.

Earnest remembered his childhood romantically. "Life in this part of the country was very nice—hunting rabbits, squirrels, possum, raccoon, fox, and others. Neighbors were wonderful to visit with and help when in need with food or work. Lots of parties, social and play parties." Earnest became defensive. "My early life would maybe seem rather drab to many people. But looking back, I would not like to change any part . . . except the loss of my mother at so early an age and that we could not get a better education. Our childhood was wonderful with all the great nature around us, and most of our living coming from the good earth."

But there were painful memories, too. I asked Earnest to describe them. He described at length the loss of his dog, Danny.

"When I was about four years old, my cousin gave me a pretty little black puppy. I named him Danny. He was always a little dog. As he grew older he would leave our yard and run down our lane toward the big road. When I would see him leaving, I would climb over a four-foot picket fence, angle across the garden lot, jump over another slat fence, catch Danny, and hold him by his body, with his feet in my face. That didn't make me turn him loose.

"I would take him into the house, put him in the small dark closet under the stairsteps, and button the door. He would stay there until my mother would find him. She would tell me I could not put Danny in the closet again. I was afraid Danny would get hurt. After a few times of me putting Danny in the closet, she began to whip me each

Gourd fiddle from Earnest's Kentucky childhood

time. All reason in me was lost. I had to put him up. This went on for weeks and months—many, many whippings could not change me.

"I never had any money. One day my father said, 'Earnest, see this nickel. I'll give it to you for Danny.' I guess I thought Danny would still be at our home. So I took the nickel. After I took the nickel Dad said, 'Earnest, Danny is not your dog anymore, and you cannot put him in the closet again.' Danny ran away, crawled up under our house and died."

Recalling the event, Earnest told me that he "about went crazy—it still hurts."

Why did Earnest dwell on this event? Why should it be significant? One reason is that it led to a comment on his response to bereavement. "The next day I carried chips and stove wood from the woodyard and stopped up all the holes in the fence, where I thought Danny could get through. I remember all the above very vividly, but I don't remember how I got over Danny's running away, unless it was my good job of filling all the escape holes." Earnest did not accept

Danny's death; the dog had "run away," he said. Earnest sought control. He threw himself into something which compensated for his grief, something which signified an activity that would change things or a least recover them as they were. He was preoccupied with carrying wood to the holes in the fence.

Earnest knew grief later in life too. His first son, born in 1935, and his third son, born in 1944, were both brain-damaged at birth. There was struggle. Earnest moved the family to a fifty-acre farm on what is now 56th Street in Indianapolis. Earnest remodeled the seventy-five-year-old house and farmed the land. He felt comfortable in his familiar farm surroundings. "This was beautiful living and eating with our beef and many vegetables and berries from our garden stored in our big freezers—butchered hogs in our smokehouse; milk, cream, butter, and cottage cheese from our cows; and honey from our bees. The farm was a wonderful place to raise children, and extra wonderful for our two retarded boys." But by 1963, both boys had died.

Around the time of their death, Earnest revived his chain carving, something he had not done since childhood. His woodcarving was inspired by a trip to North Carolina where he saw men whittling and was reminded of his past. When he began carving again, he found that it relaxed him and that urban viewers were impressed with his work. The carving helped to push uninvited thoughts about his sons out of his mind.

Not as difficult for Earnest as for other carvers, but still significant, was his adjustment to urban life.

"March 1924. I left the little community of Fairplay, Kentucky, and came to Indianapolis, Indiana. My total worth was a few work clothes in a ninety-eight-cent suitcase, new trousers, new shoes, a used dress coat, my pocketknife, and about eleven dollars.

"Fortunately, I found work at Lauters Furniture Factory. But I had trouble getting home that night, and after. I learned fast those first few weeks in the big city."

Factory work didn't agree with Earnest. After a few weeks he found work as a landscape architect, a job which brought him "closer to nature."

The balance between farm life and urban job did not last. Earnest had hoped to build a new house on his farmland and retire in 1970, but urbanization, with which he had never felt comfortable, destroyed

Earnest's belt-buckle chain

his plans. He described his disappointment, "We found our land zoned for business. The house was old and hard to keep. It was a sad day for me when I had to move away from this wonderful land." Pressured to leave, Earnest and his wife Dorothy moved to a small home with a tillable plot of land in a residential area north of Indianapolis. In the back of the house he built a workshop for his carving.

Earnest's boyhood home was gone, too. His parents were dead. Chain carving literally became his "links" to his past. The links reminded him of the value rural life places on closeness to nature and on handwork. Many people in Indianapolis, he found, had never even heard of, let alone seen, the puzzling carved chain. "Many were amazed," he explained, "that it can be done. When I was young it was thrilling to see a chain develop from a stick of wood. Now I get pleasure from showing those who are interested how to make chains with balls-in-cages and other gadgets mixed among the chain links." In response to the interest of city residents in his carvings, he spent many of his retired days demonstrating his carving to various boys' groups, especially the retarded. He thinks of this volunteer work, sharing his traditional knowledge with youth, as his "greatest contribution." He enjoys helping those like his sons, and he also hopes, like Wandley, that he can "pass it on." He wants chain carving, and the values it represents, preserved and cherished.

Earnest also collects old tools, many similar to tools he remembered from childhood. His tools completely fill a wall of his workshop. Old axes, mauls, musical instruments, and planes keep watch from over the other side of the room from where Earnest carves. Combined in one room, the carving and the tools are closely connected because they both carry in their forms and uses symbols of older rural values, one of which is the extension of oneself into nature.

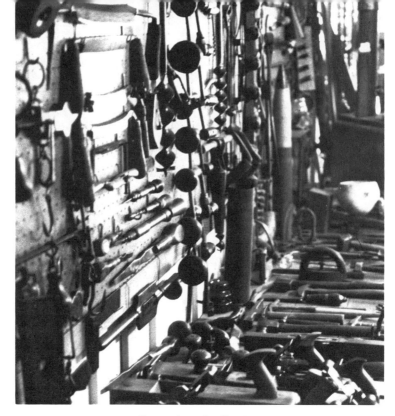

Earnest's tool collection

Because Earnest lives in a large city, he has had more opportunities than the other carvers to participate in clubs. Indianapolis clubs for woodcarvers and tool collectors have shows and demonstrations at malls and conventions. The clubs attract both those who have learned their carving traditionally, like Earnest, and those who wish to pick it up through the club. Members share a delight in crafted wood, and they have connections with clubs around the country. Cities have customarily spawned clubs catering to the many interests of their residents. The rural migrant to the city finds that he can express his traditional skills through organized clubs and festivals. Nevertheless, it strikes Earnest as strange that city dwellers should take up a tradition such as carving without knowing or experiencing the values and informal learning that, for Earnest, constitute the soul of the object. Cities do not necessarily destroy such older traditional skills, but they certainly recast them. In the city, the public face of carving becomes more unusual, specialized, and celebratory, compacted into shows, festivals, and other special occasions.

One new setting for many traditional carvers is the museum. How strange it is sometimes to see living men and women practice their crafts beside things labeled "antiques," yet how refreshing it is to see artifacts come alive. Earnest and his wife occasionally demonstrate for the Indianapolis Children's Museum. Sitting in front of a painted backdrop of a rural setting, Earnest shows his carving and tools. Inside a restored log house nearby sits Dorothy, quietly quilting. A rustic fence worms across the area protecting Earnest from visitors. Spotlights raise sweat on his brow. People take notice. Impatient mothers, antsy children, sluggish fathers, wide-eyed college students. He notices them, for their attention tells him that his past lives yet. His creativity captures imaginations still. He tries to explain that it's not always easy for him; trying to extend himself by making variations on the chain design can have its frustration. But like making music for the musician, or making images for the poet, the obstacles and the occasional emptiness can give way to an elated spirit when creativity blossoms. Maybe Earnest and his wife are transitional figures in modern attitudes toward creativity. He wouldn't have known such public notoriety back in Fairplay, but he might have felt that his carving was more integrated with his surroundings and life around him.

As Earnest carved on the stage representing his childhood, a small child stood on his own stage, even though it wasn't labeled as such. From Earnest's side the harsh lights and pale floors seemed artificial. But when the boy touched a chain he made, their stages met. The boy asked him, "Mister, how do you do this?" Earnest smiled as he answered the child, for he felt that part of his life would be illuminated by this explanation of chain carving. And he passed on another lesson to the child, "We have had a wonderful life and we're still working at it."

OBJECTS OF EXPERIENCE

George, Floyd, Wandley, and Earnest carved in old age, fueled by memories of childhood. Sometimes watching another carver or feeling a particular emotion brought memories of their hands releasing a chain or caged ball from wood. People use objects, especially handmade ones, to remind them of related sets of feelings and experiences. Writer Harriette Arnow captured the mood of handcarving well in her novel *The Dollmaker*. Gertie, the dollmaker, came from her native

Kentucky to alien Detroit. Whittling, "foolishness" she took for
granted, became her support and part of her means of holding onto
the past. "She sat again and tried to whittle," Arnow wrote of Gertie, "but thought instead of hens clucking over eggs, sage grass burn-
ing at twilight, the good taste of the first mess of wild greens, and
early potatoes going into the ground. Potatoes? Good Friday was late
enough for the first beans, and in this week was Good Friday. Hands,
knife, and doll dropped into her lap together. She had known."[16] And
when she thought that her Reuben was killed, she turned to her knife
and wood. Her husband misunderstood, though. "Aw Gert, you've
set up all night a worken on that thing," he scolded. "What a you
want to take all that trouble to whittle out them logs, when you could
ha made th cross flat out a little boards in a third a th time." But
the time spent, slowly and carefully, on the wood was time spent
on reshaping herself.

Play dramatizes experiences and feelings on a safe stage. Play with
objects works further to materialize the props and settings which act
as personal and social symbols for the actor. Play attracts others to
your creation. Maybe they'll understand. Even if they don't you can
still feel a sense of accomplishment, for they took notice, didn't they?
Aldous Huxley's John Bidlake, the old master painter relegated to the
past, knew that in the novel *Point Counter Point*. Viewers look at
his painting with eyes open but hearts closed. "It's good," one man
says. "It's enormously good. Look at the way it's composed. Perfect
balance, and yet there's no suggestion of repetition or artificial arrangement." Then we learn, "The other thoughts and feelings which
the picture had evoked in his mind he left unexpressed. They were
too many and too confused to be easily put into words. Too melan-
choly above all; he did not care to dwell on them." They were looking at a playful scene of bathers, and Huxley reminds us, "What remained of John Bidlake, the John Bidlake of five and twenty years
ago, was there in the picture too. Another John Bidlake still existed
to contemplate his own ghost. Soon even he would have disappeared.
And in any case, was he the real Bidlake . . . ? And real Bidlake, their
creator, existed by implication in his creatures."[17]

When Earnest grasped the chain he made when he was twelve,
he thought of the colors and the smells of the hills and woods of his
boyhood, and, by implication, the values and beliefs he held then.
Wandley Burch kept his father's anvil, which brings back memories

of life in his father's blacksmith shop. George Blume buttressed his identity and security by carving things reminiscent of his boyhood village. Their carvings made solid and tangible their fading recollections, and they captured ideas in shapes.

The carvings are removed from the everyday, so they can encapsulate the special meanings of the everyday. They can be felt, and provide feelings; they can be held out at arm's length or close to the heart. Talking about art and ritual, anthropologist Victor Turner pointed to how during celebrations, "people think and feel more deeply than in everyday life. They express the meanings and values of their societies in special, often vivid ways. Among these is the creation of beautiful or striking objects, which exist only because humankind celebrates its own existence."[18] Carvers celebrate—or—display their experience through their objects, but that celebration is not always joyous and triumphant. Carvers mark sorrow and pain, also. Carving is itself a celebration or marking of the self, where the carver can block out troubles and also think and feel more deeply.

When one is no longer in the mainstream of life, there is a tendency to compress one's experiences it into intense activity, or even festivity. Assimilated ethnic groups hold ethnic festivals to renew their members' loyalties to ethnic roots. Tourists bring home souvenirs of their trip to remind them later of what they experienced. A charm bracelet holds trinkets that mark passages. Carving was integrated into the childhoods of the men. After retirement, they chose to do it intensively. Carving reinforced their identities and renewed their self-worth in surroundings in which they felt alienated. The shapes they made were compressed too. Why did the carvers make small rustic buildings and tools besides the chains and caged balls? They are symbolic charms, too, that mark their lives. But by making it tangible, they generalize and enlarge their experience.

The carvers thought of their lives as "traditional." In their experience, the machine, the city, the factory, were not traditional, or creative. Folklorists argue that urban and industrial folklore does exist, and they talk about the folklore of computers or suburbia. There are, after all, customs surrounding these things that are informally learned, repeated, and varied. The carvers, however, aver that their craft is founded in what they would call old-fashioned social virtues, such as "visiting," neighborliness, and faith, that the modern world does not nurture. Because their hand-made objects, such as the chain or caged ball, have been shared by people of other generations and in other locales, the object acquires social importance. The chain is associated with commonly recognized precedents and serves as a means for adjustment by, and communication among, carvers.

Some observers assume that the carver is a happy-go-lucky figure. Historian Kenneth Ames calls this the myth of the poor but happy artisan.[19] It is related to a bundle of socially held assumptions about craft and rural life. Rural life does not have the monopoly on crafts-work, but carvers have made associations—between hand and nature, craft and village—that support that assumption. Besides such associations, there are oppositions perceived between the harmony of the farm, and the disharmony of the city, the virtue of the country, and the vice of the factory. Impressed in mind, these categories are hard to deny, and they influence action and creativity. At the same time that these shared categories contribute to the perception of an opposition between a conflict-free past and a conflict-ridden present, individual experience sometimes tells otherwise. Earnest, who thought about landscape as much as craft, saw in the gently curving lines of his links the rolling countryside and its winding roads; in harshly straight shapes he felt the city's grid and artificiality. For George Blume, the chain can stand for conflict and harmony, pleasure and pain. The symbols are not mutually exclusive. Standing at a distance, the viewer may not see the mesh. With the object and maker in arm's reach, however, I learned that the chain can stand for a conflict in the past that was overcome. When a chain is made in the present the carver is reenacting that conflict, ritually overcoming it in wood.

Conflict is by no means the whole story. Simple joys can be derived from making something with one's own hands. Conceiving an idea, working natural materials, finishing and perfecting the shape, and beholding it give makers great satisfaction. The hand-made object can evoke the compassionate feeling typically elicited by touching and stroking.

A carver may not be aware of the conflicts that drive him. If he were, he may not have to carve, for he would not need to project those inner conflicts symbolically. But carvers apparently not driven by conflicts do carve, which suggests other motives, indeed a complex web of motives. A desire to reduce conflict, to help adjustment, and relax the muscles and nerves, are strong motives. Another that came out in the stories I heard from the carvers is the desire to encapsulate their experience. Carving those expeiences as small, compact symbols and having others like what they did made them feel that what they went through was good. They mattered.

Chain carving goes beyond constructing objects only of utility, for some objects are playful. As play, carving allows the carver to experiment, to try out creative options. George Blume made a wheel that was powered by flowing sand; Earnest Bennett carved a belt buckle across a chain; Floyd Bennington challenged hardwoods; and Wandley Burch used barn boards for carving wood. Making a chain toyed with reality by temporarily offering problems and resolving them in wood; making a chain provided physical and emotional escape by replacing real-life problems. And although the carver may play down the importance of the object, the denial itself can reveal the real significance of the object to its creator. "The lady doth protest too much!"

The accounts given by carvers are similar, yet very different. They speak to the ideas that people currently share about wooden chains, and the capacity of hand-made objects to be personalized, to mean something particular about a moment or place for a certain maker or viewer. Familiar with woodworking, the men celebrated their rural pasts and their folk knowledge through carving. As they carved, they commented on the changing world presently around them and its conflicts with their way of doing things. As they talked, their unique personalities and experiences came through their carvings too.

As our society defines the life span, the carvers are old. They have an acute need at their age for creativity, maybe even more so than at other times in their lives, to stay productive and to feel worthwhile. For George, Floyd, Wandley, and Earnest, chain carving was an appropriate and satisfying form of creative expression. It was masculine, productive, and attractive. It brought out their creativity and drew others to them. It could be worked on alone yet used to reach others. It was something they thought they did well.

The links the carvers made reach back into their past. Commonly when I heard the men talk about themselves, they checked their pocketknives, waiting to give dimensions to their values and experiences. They also gave expression to their present needs and conditions. "Part of you is in a carving, see; there's something there that goes with it" is Floyd's romantic way of rephrasing George's playful

"I went through a lot of bull and I made a lot of bull." Playful and serious, romantic and conflicting, the carved chain sings loudly in the choir of the men's carvings. The carved chain sings for its quiet composer. What the voices of the men don't reveal, their objects do, but it took their voices to bring the objects to life.

Bet You Don't Know How I Made This

"SO YOU'RE interested in woodcarving, huh? Well, I got something you'll like for sure," Wandley Burch said.

He appeared reserved, yet confident. He reached for a foot-long poplar chain with caged balls on either end. He draped it around his neck, grinned, and then handed it to me.

"Bet you don't know how I made this!" he suddenly beamed.

No glue or screws held the links. No seam or hidden joint surfaced. The links flowed. My eyes followed their lines as easily as if they were a river's current. The chain was, as carvers like to boast "made out of just one piece of wood." I held in my hands a puzzle as much as a carving. My curiosity to know how things are made and how they work was aroused. I stretched the links and shook the balls trapped in the cages. I thought, as I was supposed to, "How are those links connected?" and "How did he get those balls in there?"

No two of Wandley's chains match exactly, but similarities exist. The chains usually measure from one to three feet. They have rough rectangular links made out of aged poplar. George Blume, on the other hand, prefers pine to poplar, smooth ovals to rugged rectangles. His chains sometimes run as long as twenty feet.

The carved chain is a result of a technical procedure the maker has mastered and personalized. Having figured out the trick and with completed chain in hand, he becomes a trickster. The chain represents more than a form to be admired: it shows style, persistence, ability. The carved chain embodies knowledge.

Earnest Bennett's hook, swivel, snake, pivot, and hinge

Once the skill is mastered, how many variations are possible? Wandley had pliers also made out of one piece of wood, but Wandley, like Floyd Bennington, did not normally adorn his chains, except for an occasional hook or caged ball. George Blume, however, added joints, swivels, hooks, and caged balls. Earnest Bennett went even further with his chains.

"You want to see what can be done with a wooden chain?" Earnest dared me.

"Sure," I answered, wondering what he had in store for me.

He presented a carved chain unlike any I had seen. It was a concatenation of imaginative designs that made me marvel. There was, for instance, a hook that pivoted on a barbell that was wrapped by a snake. The barbell could swing to and fro on a swivel attached to a sliding joint with four bars.

"I'm not quite finished with it," Earnest apologized.

"What will you add?" I asked incredulously.

"There's a wooden belt buckle, twisted links, and several balls in one cage that's real interesting to put on. If you can make a chain and cage, the rest are just variations on the trick."

While the complexity of Earnest's chain dazzled, the simplicity of Floyd Bennington's chains charmed. His finishes were smooth as silk, his lines as graceful and precise as a ballet dancer's steps. Viewers held his chain of three polished links gently, as they would precious gems. "How do you do it?" they would ask, "How do you get it so fine, so perfect?"

"I like to work on it," he would simply reply.

The making of the chain fascinates the carvers and sometimes holds even more satisfaction than the completed object itself. They learn the formula and add touches that express their particular tastes. Each link made is practice for the next or preparation for a new design springing from the chain.

As Earnest and Wandley carved, the repetition inherent in the scene was appealing, soothing. The pocketknife drops shavings to the floor. The carver stops to feel the texture of the wood. He blows away sawdust and strokes the finish. His eyes move meticulously along the length of wood. With more cuts and pokes the outline of a link emerges. His gaze fixes on the remaining obstacles to the link. He slices the wood gingerly at just the right place, and, suddenly, the link releases. He smiles, ready for the next one, and the one after that. Links fall over his palm as the chain takes shape.

In the carver's decisions and preferences, aesthetics can be discerned. Each carver conveys himself as he talks about his unique version of the proper appearance of the chain and way of making it. Sharing the attraction to the chain's shape, though, the carvers have in common principles that guide them toward the finished product. Complete, the chain becomes part of a drama between maker and viewer. On the street, it is given to friends and family, used to delight children or impress other workers. When the maker is removed, as in the gallery and museum, there are different kinds of viewers and different views. Back on the carver's bench, the carver contemplates the things he makes. Beside the chains often lie pliers, caged balls, fans, animal figures, and puzzles. What connects them, and what attracts the maker and viewer to them?

These questions command the attention of this chapter. The answers help shed light on what I call "folk technics"—manual skills and procedures learned traditionally for the creation of objects or the completion of tasks. Folk technics describe how things are designed, worked, and completed, especially when done for local use. Oriented toward process, folk technics involve tools and materials used, formulas and variations practiced, aesthetics and principles applied, viewers and their reactions, and the maker's repertoire.

TOOLS

"First, you need a good knife," Floyd Bennington said, echoing the traditional wisdom of the proverb "A worker is as good as his tools." Floyd and the other whittlers avoided the specialized carving tools of the sculptor. They preferred the humble folding pocketknife, also called a jackknife. Portable and useful, it connotes to some a sense of ingenuity and industriousness. In an autobiography published in 1856, for instance, Samuel Goodrich recalled his early days of making toys and household articles for his family and friends with his pocketknife. This memory led him to ask, "Why is it that we in the United States surpass all other nations, in the excellence of our tools of all kinds?" "Because," he answered, "we have in early life, this alphabet of mechanics theoretical and practical—whittling."[1] Although this mechanics is not uniquely American, it raises images common in American iconography of the versatile, rugged, and resourceful man working in the woods.

The pocketknife challenges the carver to demonstrate his full abilities. The pocketknife makes carving more of a fair fight between man and material. After wresting a design from the drab block of wood, the carver can boast, "That's all handmade."

Using the pocketknife transports the carvers back in time. A boy growing up in southern Indiana in the early twentieth century received his first knife usually from his father, who demonstrated the proper handling of the prized item to the youngster. Floyd Bennington's remark, "A boy was lost without his pocketknife," was retold by other carvers who pointed out the versatility and portability of the tool for everyday duties. Besides cutting chores, boys used the knife for several games like "mumblety-peg" and "stretch." Possession of the knife was a status symbol for the young Hoosier male, enabling him to begin learning the masculine use of tools. He could show off creative skills to his peers, often in imitation of his elders.

The young boy could also emulate literary and media masculine heroes. Huckleberry Finn's exploits with his pocketknife caught youngsters' imagination, and, as another example, radio hero Jack Armstrong in the 1930s offered knives to children on every show. Popular boys' and men's magazines in the early twentieth century often included as demonstrations of manual skill descriptions of chain carving done with a pocketknife.[3] A boy's interest might also be

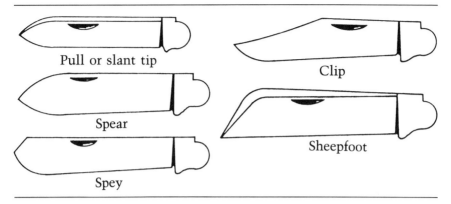

Blade styles

aroused by tales of remarkable whittling abilities of elder family members or neighbors. As a child, Wandley Burch heard about a whittler who could take a matchstick and "get a half a bushel of shavings off of it" with a pocketknife!

Pocketknives appear in many sizes and shapes. The common pocketknife used for whittling may contain from one to four blades, which fall into several types. The *clip* blade has a long, curved cutting edge for general cutting and reaching into restricted areas. The *sheepfoot* provides a straight cutting edge with a curve at the tip to add strength. *Spear points* are often found in thin penknives and are used for cutting in small or delicate areas. The *spey tip* looks like the mirror image of the sheepfoot; the spey has its cutting edge on the curve, thus making it useful for cutting roundbottomed grooves and for smoothing out wood. In addition, *pull* blades, or what carvers sometimes call *slant tips*, resemble the sheepfoot but are usually thinner and more supple.[4]

Carvers often supplement their store of pocketknives with homemade knives for special uses. Earnest Bennett shaved a piece of steel to a small spear point and added it to a wooden handle. It makes tiny cuts in chains made out of matchsticks. Similarly, Floyd Bennington shaped a curved knife for rounding out corners in his chain links and caged balls. He tapped the old rural tradition of constructing handtools for specific tasks when specialized tools were unavailable.

Today, chain carvers may speed up the process by using modern

Two of Floyd Bennington's knives: left, a commercially made knife;
right, homemade knife

power and hand tools. Wandley Burch roughs out blocks of wood with
power saws and drills holes to open areas with drill presses. But he
always completes the wooden chain with pocketknives. George
Blume made extensive use of a coping saw to shape the wood and
of a file to smooth the wood's edges. The carvers' use of such tools
often differs from their childhood imitation of older men who relied
solely on the pocketknife. Some contemporary carvers, such as Willie
Hausmann of St. Philip, Indiana, however, insist on employing only
pocketknives so as to highlight their skill and patience with the single
hand tool.

Basic accessories to the carver's knives are the whetstone and the
leather strop. The whetstone, usually made out of Washita, typically contains two grains, coarse and medium, for sharpening the blades.
The carver puts an oil mixture on the stone's surface to lift and carry
metal particles off the stone's grain. As a result of sharpening on the
whetstone, the knife has a "wire-edge," which the carver can smooth
by rubbing the blade on a buffed leather strop in barbershop fashion.

Carvers spend much time and energy sharpening their blades.
Keeping them sharp makes cutting easier and safer since the blade
is less prone to slip. Floyd Bennington and Earnest Bennett mentioned
a traditional test for a blade's sharpness. They scrape their forearms
with the knife; if they can easily cut their arm hair, the knife is ready.
The mark of a conscientious carver, woodworkers will tell you, is
the attention paid to the sharpness of his tools.

Wandley Burch's basement workshop

No specialized shop or work area is necessary for the carver's work. The portability of the pocketknife allows the carver to work in almost any location. Earnest Bennett used to whittle when he had to wait for his son at work. Wandley Burch carved chains during breaks from his job. Others like George Blume and Floyd Bennington carve in their workshops which are separate from the rest of the house. Such allocation of space suggests a masculine learning model, for it continues the notion that the home is the woman's domain and the area outside, beneath, or above the house is the man's. The early training on the pocketknife was, in part, also a learning model for the masculine possession of tools and social skills necessary for the boy to develop a facility for repairing, manipulating, and crafting.

MATERIALS

Carvers choose their woods carefully, for the difficulty of the carving and the appearance of the final product depend on the type of wood used. Carvers look for woods that are durable, attractive, tractable, and accessible. Chain carvers in southern Indiana commonly use white pine, sugar pine, yellow poplar, basswood, and cedar. These woods possess the pleasing appearance and easy workability that carvers seek. Wandley Burch prefers to make miniature pliers from pine because of its "tougher grain," but he makes his chains out of old yellow poplar, a smooth-grain wood that he takes from abandoned barns because "it just looks a little bit better—you got a story to it, you know. The house is real old." Indeed, many carvers used scrap wood from old buildings and fence posts for its nostalgia and its free and easy availability.

Particular characteristics of certain woods appeal to different carvers. Willie Hausmann, the man from St. Philip who carved the Reverend Ken Scherry's remarkable chain, enjoyed the pungent aroma of cedar, but Floyd Bennington thought cedar too brittle for his liking. He occasionally carved cherry, a wood usually regarded as difficult to work, to show off his skill. He also like the distinctive reddish-brown color and close grain. Similarly, Wandley Burch sometimes carved redwood, when he could get it, for its warm reddish-brown color.

The length of the chains is generally determined by the size of the solid piece of wood. Because most carvers use scrap wood, which comes in small sections, the chains tend to be short. Small pieces of wood also offer the advantages of portability and easy handling, and divide the work into quickly finished units. There is a point of diminishing returns: Earnest Bennett carries wooden kitchen matches to carve chains, which takes a slow, masterly hand. The carver may whittle on whatever is at hand. "In my boyhood days," one carver remarked, "a common sight was older men getting together for a chat, at which time they were very apt to reach into their pocket and get out their knives; then look around for a stick or some wood to idly carve while they talked."[5] Because space is often at a premium in carvers' homes, small sections of scrap wood also have the advantage of easy storage.

Most chains I saw in southern Indiana were six to twelve inches long and were made of poplar or pine. These woods "split out" straight and smooth when cut and are sufficiently soft so as not to crack ahead of the blade. The woods are strong and heavy enough, however, to withstand handling while the carver proceeds to make new links on the chain. The straight grains of these woods are conducive to the carving of chains and caged balls because these carvings require mostly uniform and rectilinear cuts. Several carvers complained, however, that the quality of woods available now is inferior to those used years ago.

Chain carving demands knowledge about the characteristics of different woods, knowledge more widely held in the past, before the modern technological revolution, when many implements were made by hand out of wood. Many elderly carvers still remember when their knowledge of the woods used in everyday activities was extensive. Carving was connected to recognizing and using the natural landscape. This point hit home when I visited Edward Hausmann, cousin of dead carver Willie Hausmann, in St. Philip, Indiana. He lamented the inability of youngsters to recognize the appearances and characteristics of local woods. "There were some boys out here and they couldn't even tell the difference between, or even *see*, poplar or elm or cedar," he told me. He was surprised, unsure of how boys can get by without pulling out a pocketknife and cutting themselves some berries for eating or a branch for whittling. Like the chain carvers, Ed Hausmann grew up in and continues to live a way of life that requires the knowledge of woods and the means to work them. Chain carving teaches and demonstrates that knowledge.

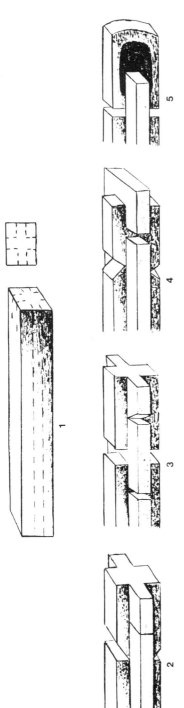
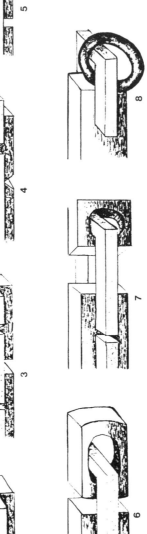
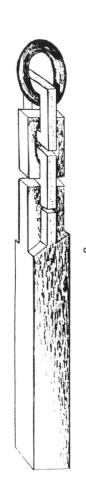

Steps in making a chain

FORMULAS AND VARIATIONS

Cutting a chain out of a solid block of wood involves taking risks, which increase if variations are tried. The wood must not crack, and the chain must not end up looking sloppy or bizarre. For a chain to be a success, viewers have to accept it as a chain. Carvers reduce risk and error by following set procedures—formulas in their heads worked by their hands. Following the formulas ensures consistency, while allowing leeway for variation. Formulas allow the carver to concentrate more on style and shape than on figuring out how to proceed. Having a formula encourages action.

The carver begins working within a defined set of choices from the moment he picks up his knife, traditionally relying on a limited number of grips. In the *forehand grip*, the carver holds the handle of the knife in a clenched fist with his thumb stretched out under the handle and he holds the wood behind the blade with his other hand. He moves the blade away from his body in long cutting strokes to remove large slivers of wood. The *draw grip* offers the carver more control; he holds the wood with one hand in front of the blade while his clenched fist grasps the knife. His thumb anchors the back end of the wood, and he makes short cuts toward his body. The *pointer grip* resembles the forehand grip except that the carver places his thumb on the back of the blade for leverage to provide added force and control. The carver uses the *dagger grip* to make deep cuts. He presses down on the wood with one hand while his fist holds the knife at a forty-five-degree angle to the wood. He places his thumb on the end of the handle for leverage while moving the knife toward his body. In the *pencil grip*, as the name implies, the carver holds the knife like a pencil and cuts toward the body. This grip is useful for precise cuts and detail work.

Having gripped his knife, the carver can make seven basic types of cuts: wedge, seesaw, slice, stop, saw, drill, and scrape.[6] In the *wedge cut*, the carver cuts and splits the wood fiber by placing the long edge of the blade against the wood and moving the blade down a desired distance. In the *seesaw cut*, the carver magnifies the wedging effect by rocking the blade back and forth across the wood. Like the wedge cut, the *slice cut* is used to cut slivers of wood, but as the blade cuts, the carver moves the knife back from the tip to the handle in a slicing motion. The *stop cut* outlines a cut in the wood by placing the tip of the blade in the wood at a right angle to it and then

(Opposite, above, and right)
Wandley cuts around a link
and releases it

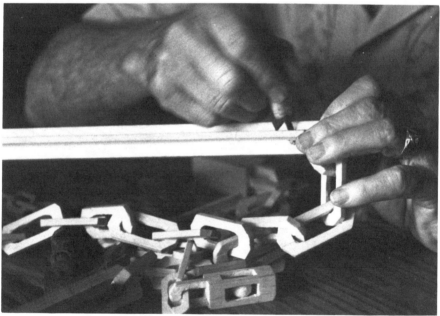

(Opposite and above) Earnest making a chain

tilting the knife slightly to make a cut. The *saw cut* has a back and forth action to cut through small sections of wood. In the *drill cut*, the carver places the tip of a clip, spear, or slant-tipped blade at a right angle to the wood and by rotation and pressure makes a small hole in the wood. In the *scrape cut*, the carver holds the blade at about seventy-five degrees to remove surface fiber, often to lift tool marks from the wood. Of course, the carver may vary the delineated grips and cuts to mark, split, cut, gouge, and smooth the wood according to the demands of the specific problem at hand and the technical preferences of the carver. Knowledge of the terms for the cuts varies from carver to carver. He often knows the types and uses of different cuts without having specific labels for them.

The limited combinations of grips and cuts are conducive to making chains because the chains require removing long sections of wood, followed by incisive and precise cuts to release and smooth the links. Most carvers follow the same steps to carve the basic chain. First, the carver chooses a rectangular piece of wood, usually no more than three inches wide, and he marks two parallel lines on each side of the wood, thus dividing the sides into three sections. On the end of the block the carver outlines the form of a cross. Using a combination of slice and stop cuts, the carver removes wood to form a cross-shaped length of wood. He then makes small v-shaped grooves in the edges of the wood to outline the outer borders of the links. Then by using drill and slice cuts, the carver removes wood from the area at the center of the link. He is careful not to crack the protruding piece of wood that will form the second link. By cutting down on the area of contact between the first and second link, the carver releases the links from each other. Then he smooths the corners of the released rectangle to form a polished oblong link. The carver proceeds similarly down the length of the wood until he has freed all the links.

The carver can embellish his chain with a variety of shapes by leaving a section of wood uncut in the length of the wood. A common addition, for example, is the caged ball. The carver usually puts this rectangular addition at the ends of his chain, for the caged ball represents a separate technical problem that requires a formula different from that of the chain. The human eye, in viewing a rectilinear form, such as a chain or, for that matter, a sentence, is attracted especially to the beginning and to the end of the composition. Yet such flanking of the chain by shapes that contrast with it helps draw attention to the chain itself, and the overall impression is one of balance and pleasing design. In their own way, carvers match a prevalent Western tendency to arrange art and architecture bilaterally and symmetrically.[7]

As well as pleasing the eye, the chain and caged balls puzzle the mind. You want to figure out how the links connect without a break in the wood. And of the caged ball, you can't help ask, "How the hell did that ball get in there?" To make a caged ball the carver uses a square or rectangular section of wood. He makes an outline of a cage's bars on all four sides and marks a small square in the center of the cage where the ball or balls will be. He gouges wood away from around the ball until he has open spaces on either side of the ball area. Then he rounds out the ball and cuts down between the ball and the cage's pillars to free the ball. This can be tricky because rounding the ball requires cuts against the grain. By applying the formula for making caged balls, the carver can make variations on the basic form, just as he would with the links of the chain. Variations include several balls in a cage, monkey or dog in a cage, chains on shafts (reverse ball-in-cage), balls in a cylindrical or hexagonal cage, cages with five

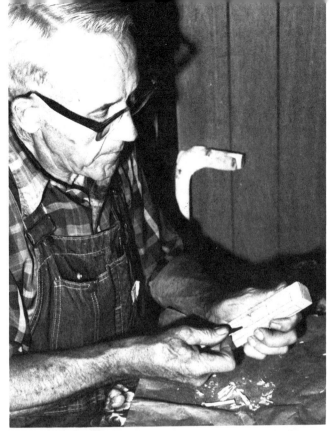

(Left and below)
Wandley starts a
caged ball

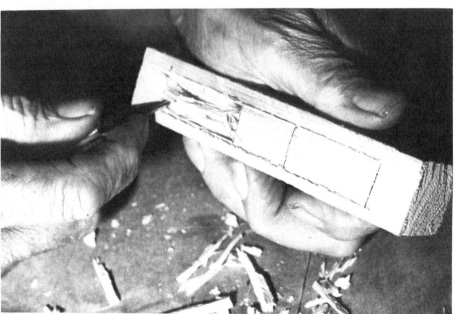

(Left and below)
Wandley cuts
through cage
and shapes ball

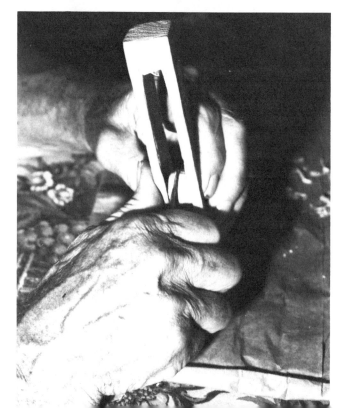

Wandley releases the ball

(or six, seven, or eight) pillars, and cages with grilles. By a related procedure of outlining and cutting away excess wood, the carver can add joints, swivels, hooks, and anchors to the chain.

Making chains and cages involves a repetitious and predictable formula that allows creative variation within a structured design. By employing the formula, the carver controls error and reduces risk while attempting unprecedented patterns. Earnest Bennett, while working within the conventions of the traditional formula, experimented with the novel additions of a wooden belt buckle and a snake to his chain. Following the chain formula thus allowed him a range of creative choices including the arrangement of objects within the chain and the alteration of the size, shape, and length of the chain. He can ensure that the basic forms he uses will be recognized by his audience, yet he maintains an outlet for innovation and personal expression.

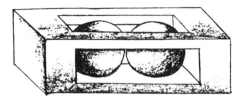

Double caged ball

Ball in a twisted cage

Dumbbell (reverse ball-in-cage)

Heart on shaft

Sliding joint

Spoon with caged
balls and chain

Variations of caged ball

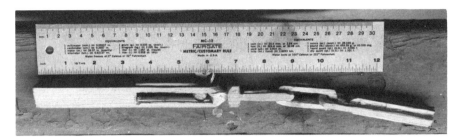

Wandley's caged ball, swivel, and links

Not only can the carver make additions to the chain, but he can also vary the form of the chain itself. For instance, the "endless chain" is one in a circle, which poses an additional puzzle to the carver's audience: How did the carver get all the links together in a closed loop? The carver accomplishes this effect by outlining the chain in a form of a rectangle, rather than in a length, on a board. The carver can also vary the chain's form by smoothing his links into ovals, hearts, or circles or by forming twisted links, interlocking rings, and side-by-side links.

Carvers base the forms of their wooden creations on models in the real world. Carvers often showed me wooden chains which they identified specifically as watch chains, handcuff chains, fence chains, and log chains. Similarly, the hooks, swivels, and joints are based on utilitarian objects. Yet the carving can take on a fantastic quality, distinct from its utilitarian model. It is intentionally unusual. Carvers emphasize the distinctiveness of the chain by not painting them a color matching the metal-chain model. "You want the natural wood to show, so they'll know how you did it; so they'll see the wood," George Blume explained, and other carvers agreed. And so I better understood the exclamation by Gertie in *The Dollmaker*, " 'Paint?' Gertie cried. 'Cover up that pretty wood?' and she put the forkful of salmon salad she had lifted to her mouth back onto her plate."[8]

Knowing the formula is no guarantee you will be able to carve a chain. You need patience and, carvers will tell you, a certain knack. Experienced chain carvers boast a steady hand and a calculating eye. To carvers, making a chain is hardly mechanical. For it to be successful, it requires feeling, an emotional involvement with the object and all it represents.

Earnest working on a chain

Judging by the phrases in the English language, a foreigner might think that more English speakers know how to carve than really do. He'll hear, "I'm whittling away at the problem," "I'm carving out an idea now," "I'm cutting against the grain," "I'm my own carver now," and "I want to carve a place for myself." These phrases show the power, security, and feeling of progress that carving gives. The carver today is a special person, one with a magician's secrets, but one with a layman's stature. Woodcarving books abound with an "anybody can do it" and "a hobby for you" attitude. Following the logic of individualized industry, they show steps and tips to get you started; diagrams set up models of production. But the carvers I met consider that coldly mechanical, foolishly measured by time and facility—and devoid of meaning. That is not what brings their work alive.

It's not the time carving takes that counts as much as doing the task. You don't clock carving; you feel it. Carvers explore the wood. They discover its rhythm and find its character. With a sharp knife and driven fingers, carvers make the wood theirs. They work a chain, they wrestle it from the possessive wood, they don't merely 'finish' it. They think about tradition and their sense of self. They recall landscapes—country and city, old and new, natural and man-made. They admire the chain emerging from nature's wooden grip.

AESTHETICS AND PRINCIPLES

Most carved chains will resemble their metal counterparts used for pulling a cart or hoisting heavy stuff. The carver lets you know, though, that his carving is different—that it is "unreal." He'll remind you that it's wood by making the most of its distinctive texture and color. He'll jog your imagination by adding a caged ball or a linked heart.

The extremes of reality and imagination are relative to standards the carver keeps in mind as he cuts. Standards? The chain should, quite simply, *look* like a chain. It is carved; it should therefore retain the qualities of wood. But because it is a carving, the carver is free to try varied designs within the bounds of what people commonly will accept as appropriate and pleasing. As an object used to impress and reach other people, the chain depends on social acceptance, be it from the carver's family, friends, viewers, or neighbors. As a creation above the usual tasks of utility, the carved chain also demands the maker's imagination and personal taste.

Designing and making involve personal choices and preferences. Answering "How do I want it to look?" depends first on the answer to "What am I able to do?" The wood presents limitations as well as possibilities. The carver usually finds the task of making a chain eased by working with 2 x 2 blocks of straight and soft wood. Straight cuts with the grain are easier than curves against the grain.

But in other ways the carver makes aesthetic decisions that project his ideas of what pleases others and himself, indeed, of what "looks right." Wandley likes a rough, rugged look to his links. Floyd wants a polished, delicate appearance. Earnest worked at a busy and intricate feel to his chains, while George enjoyed the steady repetition of portly oval links. Despite their differences, their chains all shared a form that people recognized. "That's one of them carved chains, all right," folks in southern Indiana regularly told me when I showed them photographs of the work of Wandley, Floyd, George, and Earnest.

Why has the carved chain looked so consistent over the past few centuries? How does a carver make his aesthetic choices? The carved chain lies somewhere between "real," utilitarian machinery and a work of nature. Carving a chain is making a mediation between extremes, of artificiality and reality, of man and his environment, of the individual and his society. The goal is to strike a balance to your liking between these extremes. The shapes of the chain mirror the carver's position between these points.

Carving, and other forms of creativity, become acts of affirmation. They force you to make decisions about your identity and the appearance, indeed the beauty and worth, of your objects and world. They bespeak your presence in the society, your relationship to nature. At the times carvers made chains—childhood and retirement—their relationships to society and nature were especially on their mind. During childhood they aspire to adulthood; they want to discover the form and operation of nature. During retirement, they worry about alienation from the youthful society; with free hours available to them, yet few years left, they turn to reassuring activity; they contemplate their return to nature in death, and they feel sensitively the changes that nature brings. Carving helps them find answers. By making choices about their designs, they find balance and order. They materialize their personal expression. Often the very ambiguity of the chains—useful or useless, artificial or real—is close to the feelings of the carvers. Carving, by combining ability with recognizable form, affirms a sense of past, of place, and of worth.

People make aesthetic judgements, like many other decisions, by setting up an inner dialogue. Often the debate involves "you" speaking for your personal preferences while the "other" speaks for social concerns or outside pressures.[9] They establish the boundaries and judge the standards set by precedent. Debating the choices within themselves, they then come up with a decision that suits them.

Because in chain carving, the men control the object's creation, many decisions are involved. Carvers enjoy that control and its concomitant sense of personal involvement. "Involvement" is a value, too, that separates the carver from the man who idly, indeed off handedly, picks up chain making. "When I was young," Earnest Bennett stressed, "it was thrilling to see a chain develop from a stick of wood." He continued, "I wanted to see what I could do, what was possible with my pocketknife and wood." George Blume echoed, "I made that, see, I did it to my idea. It was a log chain but I had the wood show through there."

Folk architecture can also display the mediation between artificiality and reality. In his study of middle Virginia folk housing, Henry Glassie noted the distinction between the artificial—brick, clapboard, shingle—and the natural—mud, trees. He suggested that people possess these polarities as part of a fundamental concept when they shape objects out of nature. Hence the traditional house builder works "through a problem by means of an organic dialectic of form and material adapting one to suit the other in a free manner that suggests a high regard for natural substances."[10] The mediation, the building, imposes order and balance for humans who are at once part of nature and part of culture.

The woodcarver works within the possibilites and limitations of wood, a natural substance, and declares his control by releasing a cultural form, a pleasing form—the chain—from the material. At the same time, the carver pays his respects to the natural substance by using hand tools (the artificial) that are the *natural* extensions of his body or by preserving the natural appearance of the wood.

The carved chain strikes your eye because of its ambiguity. It lies between the manufactured metal chain and a block of wood. The

carver intentionally achieves this effect by combining a real, or artificial, shape with a "natural" substance. The result questions your
categories and assumptions of real and unreal. In making a balance
between the two extremes, the carver has given the object a strong
aesthetic appeal, because it challenges the mind and the senses. Well
it should too, for carvers report that senses are heightened during the
making of the chain. "You're in tune with that wood, see; you feel
its differences in texture and you see so sharply the lines of the grain,"
Floyd Bennington told me. Creativity and aesthetic appeal are woven
around the common thread of heightened sensitivity—to shapes, colors, moods, textures, and the relationship among them.

Part of what makes the chain work, too, is its reliance on traditional Western ideas about how our objects should look. Commonly, such design stresses repetitive forms, balanced pairs, rectangular
shapes, and tactile qualities.

Repetition provides rhythm, order, and predictability and also the
basis for variation. In music, people enjoy being able to recognize a
repeated melody and listen intently for variations on the theme. People arrange things on a shelf to repeat a design. They want regularity. Sometimes that regularity is desired mentally as well as aesthetically. Steadily repeating a task, or a design, can be therapeutic.
Hence the stereotyped image of mental patients working at the
repetitive task of basket making. Repetition is used to ease the mind
in other ways. The rows of flags in front of the United Nations, the
same height and shape, lend an impression of order to the world befit-
ting the goal of the U.N. And think of the image of harmony given
by the classic picket fence, striking the eye with its whitewashed
regularity.

Repetition can give a design importance. "If it's worth saying,
it's worth saying again," teachers often told us. Businesses design their
logos—those basic repeated trademarks—so your mind will easily accept and recognize them. Repetition gives the image of unity among
parts, and in unity and the wholeness that it implies is found importance. Repetition forces us to pause and reflect on the design. "Yes
I've seen that before; I recognize it." Overdone, or overplayed, the
repeated design can lose effectiveness, but presented within limits
usually imposed socially, the repetition of a musical theme, of a family name, or a carved link implies consequence and tradition.

Repetition connotes connection, and the chain is exemplary.

Think of the importance given the *chain* of events, the World *Series*, the *consecutive* wins, and the *line* of succession. People pay attention particularly to chain letters, chain reactions, and chain stores, because they boast extra strength. The child gurgles with delight at the row of paper dolls unfurled from a plain piece of paper. But maybe the ultimate connection is "The Great Chain of Being," championed by Arthur Lovejoy as "the realization of all possiblities."

When designs repeat and are strung together, they suggest straight lines as our eyes scan the composition. Straight lines to Westerners mean order and balance. We force our children to make their letters the same height and speak straightforwardly. We avoid "uneven" and "irregular" edges. People say disparagingly, "He's crooked," "He's twisted," or "He threw me a curve." To "go straight" or to "stay in line" refers to society's idea of what appears right, regular, and proper.

Chain carvers find the repeated design of the link appealing. The eye playfully and comfortably follows the straight string of regular forms. Repeatedly making a shape encases the structure of the design in the carver's mind, thus helping him control error and letting him vary the form within limits. The carver decides when the repetition becomes boring. He can end the chain at a certain length or add a variation.

Carvers commonly design the chain with hooks or caged balls on either end. The ends contrast with the chain and give it closure. They frame the links. The design feels comfortable because of its use of balanced pairs. You can find the tendency especially in language. People talk significantly of "on the one hand . . . and then on the other"; the beginning of an essay should balance the end with the substance in the middle. We categorize pro and con, front and back, left and right, and good and bad. To be "unpaired" is to be "odd." The prevalence of this pattern has to do with the projection of bodily shape: the presence of two equal arms and hands. The manmade world, from the head of a pin to the feet of a chair, calls upon bodily design.

Westerners' love for things in threes is usually a special case of two, for two of the three elements commonly form a pair. The windows of a house are commonly placed symmetrically around a central door. In language, sentences emphasize symmetry and a favor for threes—beginning, middle, and end—yet the beginning and end are considered stronger than the middle. Our bodies again have these features. Our faces have two eyes flanking the nose, two ears flanking the head, and two legs positioned around the genitals to give an image of threes. Carvers have pairs of designs flanking the central chain, unless they want to offset the natural tendency by putting a pronounced design in the middle.

For much of American folk design, the base rectangle fulfills the demand for straight lines and pairs. The rectangle, and the square from which it grows, is shaped by the equal opposition of vertical and horizontal lines, thus forming two sides on the left and right and on the top and bottom. The model of good proportion is usually given as the Golden Oblong—three units on the long side to two on the short side. The first space most infants know is the rectangular crib, and their rooms are normally rectangular. From birth, then, people associate the rectangle with the appropriate living space. Every folk house-type in America is based on the rectangle. Our cars, documents, and painting frames typically follow suit. We don't expect paintings— or arguments—to be circular.

The rectangle accrues extra importance because the shape conforms most to our bodies, whether in the design of beds or coffins. The rectangle, starkly artificial, asserts human control on the environment. The justified margins on these very pages testify to an implicit cultural insistence on the ordered, balanced rectangular form even if it means added cost and strain. When a legislator made the suggestion a while back that the square boxing ring (the setting for battle between *two* equally matched men) should be made into a circle to reduce the corner's injurious trap, the reply was a straight-out no. Who wants to go around in circles?

If circles and ovals are unusual, often objectifying the supernatural, curving lines are commonly viewed as natural, emanating from the country landscape. To be sure, carvers make chains out of rectangluar blocks of wood. They stretch their chains out straight, giving them an even, rectilinear appearance. Made into ovals, wooden links foil the eye's expectation. The clash makes the object stand out. It seems creative, partly because the object's design appears active, and above the ordinary. Artificial and natural, man and environment, and reality and illusion converge. The caged balls are in rectangles, often paired at either end of the chain. The basic design repeats and varies. The chain holds a traditional aesthetic system assigning meaning to form.

Another important characteristic of the chain is its tactile quality. You want to reach out to touch it. It is not meant for a gallery's protection, but for the openness of your hands. Being made by *hand*, a sensuous, touching part of your body, gives it a compassionate, carefully controlled quality that people admire. To be handy is to be useful, needed, versatile, and just a bit clever. Touch also verifies reality and reinforces meaning. You want to be *in touch with reality*, reach out and *touch someone* (since talk is cheap), *grasp* ideas, experience something *first-hand*. What is called folk art or craft usually includes strong textures and tactile qualities to bring the viewer closer to the object and therefore to the maker, as it also shows the maker's involvement with the object's production.[11] The handmade thing is closer to nature, and therefore more precious.

Since showing respect for nature becomes important to achieve the aesthetic effect of carved chains, the carver also insists on fair play between him and his environment. If you're going to fool with nature, they imply, you better at least do it fairly. The carver often looks for scrap or unused wood. He normally uses "just a small pocketknife." He won't normally use glue or screws. The carved chain is a wonder because the carver made it "with his own hands without help."

Violations occur, but usually the carver makes up for them by doing something else worthy. George Blume, as I mentioned earlier, glued his links. He compensated for the violation by making unusually long or miniature lengths of chain. Another carver, from Jasper, Indiana—an aged upholsterer named Linus Herbig—looked at a broken link he had made many years back and told me, "I could have glued this joint back but that wouldn't *satisfy* me at all." But his chains conformed to the usual standards of length and material. Wandley Burch used power tools to start his chains, a violation too, but he made up for it, so he said, by making unusually stout chains and caged balls. One caged ball reached almost two feet.

Carving is something personal, something often done alone, yet it also is social, typically done to share the product with others. George Blume mostly kept his chains private, but he simultaneously imitated chain carving he had seen others do in his community. Earnest Bennett's remarkable designs are singular, solitary flights of fancy working within the conventional way of making chains, but he seeks acceptance for these innovative ideas from the group of wood-

carvers with whom he regularly meets. Earnest balances personal whims with the conforming demands of society. The carver weighs the aesthetic judgements of people who see his chains. In doing so, he also comments on his relationship to others—how tied he is to the demands and views of the audience and to his own individuality. Chain carving is a good metaphor for that, because it operates on socially derived rules and norms which have leeway built in for personal expression.

Ah, but is it art? I hear that again and again. Art is many things to many people, and often the supposedly objective researcher and the honest critic impose their ideas about art on unsuspecting creators.

I thought I should ask the carvers.

"Art? I don't know if it'd be art or what," George Blume answered with surprise.

"What is art to you? What would you call it?" I pressed.

"I didn't call it nothing. I just made the things to be making things and that's the way I run onto one thing after the other."

Making things. Doing that by hand in this day and age often sets the maker apart, even if he does not use the term *art*. From the outside, art is imposed usually to show a person who is apart either in skill or vision. Art is also imposed to elevate the status of a skill or practice. "We don't just eat, we've made cooking an art," I hear. Art, too, is often what sells, and what is distant from immediate experience. Art can imply, as well, a frivolity, and an assumption of beauty. Art is a changing social value given to frequent formal definition by upper classes.

I wanted to know the principles that underlay George's creativity. Could I find principles that were imposed from within rather than from without? I thought I could when George made a contrast between what he did at his job and what he did at home. His finger raised toward Huntingburg's smokestacks, he spoke pensively.

"I never seen nothing like art over there at the factory. What I made there was furniture: dressers, and stuff like that. That's where I got on to making that chain though. I got to thinking. Well, damn, if them other carvers can make that, maybe I can. That led to one thing after another."

I couldn't resist. I asked him, "What do you think of when you think of art then? Is a painting art? Or a piece of furniture art?"

"I never did think much about that," he admitted. "Just what *just got into my mind*, I tried to make that. There's very few things that I tried to make that I couldn't make."

George's chains are recognizably customary to others in his community, yet the objects bear his personal and often eccentric stamp. His skill and devotion to his craft was uncommon. He belonged to no formal artworld or even an informal community of local artists. But he thought and worked creatively.

His creativity flowed when he made things, but there are levels and stages to discern. First, he mentally conceived the creation of the product and proceeded to manipulate formulaically his tools and materials in order to produce a self-satisfying and socially acceptable object. He shaped and perfected the object, based on his mental image of the proper form and procedure for arriving at that image out of materials, into a customary structure and composition. Second, George showed off types of manual and perceptual skills which he compared to those of others around him. Third, the finished product was checked for its relation to his life experience and aesthetics. If it didn't pass it would be rejected. This was not an inspection for sale but an inspection for self-satisfaction.

To those who know George and his carvings, his things are creative—and maybe art to the outsider—because they show great skill and something of the maker. George's carvings were made within certain local standards of chain making. He learned them, tried to perfect them, and eventually he manipulated them. He controlled the production of his objects, he had technical standards of excellence, and he arranged designs.

George Blume was not the only one I asked about art in chain making. Wandley Burch said, "Well, you just kind of figure it out for yourself. Of course that's the way it's been done for years."

"It" to Wandley is "making the thing." "It" is traditional—shared and repeated by others—but it is personal, something you play with by yourself. "It" is creative.

Floyd Bennington used the terms *art* and *craft* when I talked to him. They were part of each other—the mixture of technical know-how and imagination. He told me, "Chain carving's something that you have to have the crafts, or you got to have the artistic designing of it. I don't know, it's just *everything*."

"What do you mean?" I urged him to continue.

"You have to see in that block what you're going to make. You're going to have to see that chain or horse or dog, whatever it is you're making. You'll have to almost be part artist to know where to cut with this, just like you have to be an artist to know where to put your brush and make your stroke with your paint brush."

Making a chain involves a sense of skill and a feeling for form, both of which can be perfected and manipulated. Its appeal to Floyd?

"It's just that I—can *you* do it. If I can't do them, then I don't want to do them—if I can't make them look like *something*. You get these links down this far, this part back here is loose, see. And I could break that way back up here but it makes all this stuff kind of out of balance then. It's just a challenge. I've always been that way about anything like that—someone brings some furniture to repair, and after I look at it a little while I tell them whether I could do it or not. And I thought—well, in the beginning somebody made it. Somebody put it together in the beginning, and if they did it in the beginning, I should be able to reproduce it."

Floyd's change of *I* to *you* in the first sentence, his reliance on precedent at the same time as his insistence on his personal involvement, shows the balance of individuality and social demands on his work. His carving, and his attitude toward it, sets him apart, even while it connects him to others.

I showed Floyd a photograph of a chain made by George Blume. "It's a plain carving," he criticized.

"How's that?" I shot back.

"It's all right, but it's not right to *me*. A carving's got to work for you. It's got to be good and it's got to be yours."

His statement expands on Wandley's, "Bet you don't know how I made this." Creative objects and the behaviors that go into making them communicate something personal within those technical and aesthetic standards carvers share. Carvers want an expressively distinctive style they can call their own. They seek a system of technical control. And that is usually the "art" part for them.

George looked at Floyd's chains.

"Nice. He figured that darn puzzle out, but it's no log chain. Mine's a log chain. His isn't long enough or fat enough, there's no hook."

George prefers his looking more like "real" chains. Floyd prefers his more "unreal," more refined. They have both perfected what they do.

Their carvings need not be compared with statues in the Vatican or tire planters to be understood as art. What their carvings need is to be understood on their own terms. What they do isn't a hobby; it is a part of their lives. It heightens their physical senses and gives material form to their aesthetic sense. It puts their creative principles to work in their society, in the world they know.

VIEWERS AND THEIR REACTIONS

In my search to uncover the techniques of chain carving, I want to know not only about those who give but those who receive. Bert King is not a carver, but an old clockmaker. He has lived in Huntingburg just up the street from George Blume for many years.

The top of the hour arrives, bringing a chorus of chimes, rings, and cuckoos. Two long chains hang from his prize clock in the living room. When the local newspaper did a story on his clocks, he had them photograph that one, chains and all. I ask him to tell me about the two chains.

"Well, George traded me one for a mower I had," Bert said. "I thought they were really something. A lot of work, a lot of craftsmanship."

Bert hesitated. "And the second?" I asked.

His eyes reddened. "George gave that to me because he knows I like them. They remind me of my early days. I'm going to leave them to my grandchildren, maybe they'll have them and know about what we value, what we did."

Bert King's reaction to George's chain is based on a past of shared values. He saw in the chain something of his own life. He draped it over his favorite clock to set the object he had made within a certain time frame. Bert's treatment of the chain reflected a yearning for tradition and continuity.

Lil Blemker, who first put me on to chain carvers, has a chain and a darkened caged ball that sit in her cozy kitchen. She loves "antiques" for the atmosphere they create of rustic harmony. To her, chains and caged balls have the same charm and beauty as a graciously aged oak dresser or a well-wrought jug. Lil doesn't always know the carvers of her treasured items, but their presence is felt.

George Blume's daughter Patty has a chain her father made years ago, which is tucked away in the attic of her house. For her the chain evokes family memories. It is Christmas with his handmade fence around the tree, and his always making things. Carvers commonly make things for their families. The objects tie them together more closely, for the recipients share a name and the carved chain is as symbolic of certain moments in the family history, a symbolic object as expressive as the family quilt or a bronzed pair of baby shoes. Patty doesn't display the chain, but she wants it for her children's trunk of grandfather's things. The family accepts the carved item in a mood of calm expectation.

Bert, Lil, and Patty are part of the audience for chain carvers. The carver reaches out and offers, or leaves, the chain. He may get goods in return, but more often he gives simply for the satisfaction of giving and the attention it brings to him and his work. The carver does not have to be present for the sharing of the object to continue to bring pleasure to those involved in its exchange. Lil shows the aged caged ball to her daughter, who shows it to her friends. The carving creates a setting and a mood.

Dorothy Bennett wears a chain bearing a family connection. Earnest Bennett made her a wooden chain bracelet with a heart attached. It is a bond between them. In exchange, she made him a quilt. Like O. Henry's "Gift of the Magi," their creative gifts show love by giving something that comes dearly.

Still another reaction is more sensuous. At a faculty reception, I had set out some wooden chains on a coffeetable. From across the room, I saw a woman handling the chains back at the table. At first she fingered them gingerly and then animatedly. She turned to another guest and remarked, "My God, but these are fun to look at and hold!" She enjoyed the wooden texture, the way the chain formed different designs on the table as she moved links around, and the way it fell into one hand from the other.

Wandley Burch plays on that appeal when he introduces his objects with, "Bet you don't know how I made this!" By holding his chains out like exotic candies, he makes his viewers focus on the object. Grasping the object, viewers ask questions. Wandley has their attention.

At the Indianapolis Children's Museum, Earnest Bennett takes the lead in the drama of carver and viewer. Earnest usually draws a

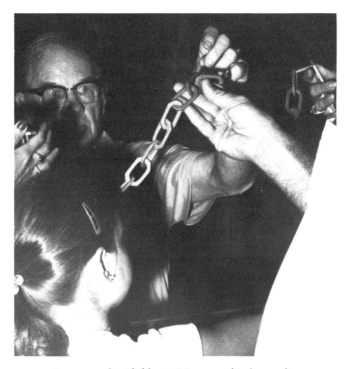

Earnest at the Children's Museum of Indianapolis

crowd by brandishing a small pocketknife and releasing links from wood. People stop to see the duel between a man's simple tool and the wood. He stops and holds it up, tempting the children to touch it. As they gently finger the links, you can hear "Neat" or "Wow," or "How do you do that Mister?"

Dorothy's quilting nearby attracts attention more visually. People admire the pattern and precision, but they don't talk about the magic or puzzle of the quilt. The fight between tool and wood appears more aggressive and risky than the meeting of needle and fabric. The quilt is pictorial and flat; the chain is figurative, multi-dimensional; and puzzling.

The carver can heighten the drama between him and the viewer by presenting the chain and caged ball as a riddle, a puzzle. Sometimes the carving does it for him. The links, coming from a single block of wood, should not be able to connect without some break between them. The ball inside the cage rattles freely, although there is no indication of how it "got in there."

Earnest shows his matchstick chain

Riddles are usually thought of as speech and confined to children at play. But riddling in the abstract and in the concrete object occurs commonly. There are better definitions of riddles than the process of riddling, even though riddling carries the burden of meaning.[12] Riddling is playful yet has some serious functions. Riddling presents apparent contradictions and asks the listener or, in the case of chains, the viewer to resolve them. Riddling challenges categories, and by doing that challenges order. When made concrete, as in the puzzle or chain, riddling also involves the senses. It forces the eye to explain an apparently illogical construction by bringing in the hand to work through the problem. The mind searches through techniques and analogies that could explain the solution. The riddler has a special knowledge that puts him above the viewer. The viewer is being ritually tested, but he engages because of the frame of play and because he hopes to show his wits by figuring out the answer.

Riddles, like other forms of play, are deeply symbolic for the originator of the riddle, as well the person trying to answer. Ambiguity characterizes riddles, and the carvers, in retirement, have much ambiguity in their lives. The viewer is posed with the task of pinpointing the sources of ambiguity in the riddle and resolving them. Roger Abrahams and Alan Dundes identified puzzles as a special type of riddle because "puzzles concentrate upon the riddlee more than any other kind of enigmatic question. He not only serves as a reflector for the wit of the riddler, but also must attempt to come up with an answer."[13] In the case of the carved chain, the answer is often provided, and the carver retains the special knowledge and superiority of the riddler, but the viewer is still a reflector. The viewer is still forced to grasp the opposition of categories that exist in the chain and caged ball. The viewer must accept that all is not what it appears to be, that looks are deceiving, and that *the old and traditional still have power and control.* Many do walk away with that subtle but powerfully delivered message. Recall George Blume's confrontation with workers at the factory: "I didn't know you could do that! If I had known that I would have come around!" they respond. They acknowledge his worth through the object that intrigues them. At the time he brought the chain to the factory, he was adapting to a change in status at his workplace, to an acceptance of aging.

In constructing the chain, he also built categories to transcend. Anthropologist Ian Hamnett reminds us that "the ability to construct categories and also to transcend them is central to adaptive learning, and riddles can be seen as a very simple paradigm of how this ability is attained."[14] Carved chain in hand, the old carver has his introduction to those who don't share his ideals. He faces children, whom he likes to delight and teach. He faces those who don't share his background, so that he might boast of his ability and experience. He can also face those who do share his ideals, like George Blume giving Bert King the second chain. Then the object speaks less in riddling tones and more in those of a proverb giving some universal truth.

The carver uses riddles, or proverbs, because his messages go deep, and therefore they involve risks. Riddling through his puzzling object is a ritual to simultaneously conceal and reveal those messages: conceal because they can be disturbing if met head on, and reveal because they are important to convey to ensure the carver's self-worth and ideal. Humor surrounding the riddling reduces the risks of

Watts Towers, Los Angeles, built by Sam Rodia (1879-1965)

Opposite, rocking chair made by Chester Cornett, Kentucky, 1965-66

broaching an uncomfortable topic. Humor also beckons the viewer to him. "Here's something funny, all right," Wandley says. Funny, strange? "Go ahead, take a look at; take it if you want." The messages will stay with the viewer. The solutions to the puzzle may be different the next time the viewer pulls out the chain. It may no longer be a technical solution, but an emotional one, for he remembers the old man who challenged the viewer's logic and learning.

Riddling pervades many objects that combine contradictory images. For the scholar of African art Robert Plant Armstrong, all works of affecting presence, of which I count the carved chain and caged ball, "exist in a state of ambiguity, for if they own presence, if they are of the nature of a person—which is what our behavior toward them argues—they are also of the nature of a thing."[15] Much publicity has been given, for example, to the mystery and evocation of Sam Rodia's "Watts Towers" in Los Angeles. They are colorful metal and concrete spirals standing in contrast to their rectangular built environment.

The towers draw attention to a maker and his special language of
form, but conceal his deeper intent.[16] I also think of the striking
rocking chair Michael Owen Jones was given by Kentucky chairmaker
Chester (Charley) Cornett. It had four rockers with bookcases on the
side, drawers underneath, five panels forming the back and sides, and
walnut pegs carved in a pattern of ridges and grooves on top.[17] The
chair was "strange" and "puzzling," Jones reported. It was ambiguous;
it didn't fit his normal idea of "chair." It forced questions to its
viewers, and demanded answers. Jones later suggested solutions.
Charley, Jones said, projected his puzzled moods in the strange rocking chair. The enclosed design matched, among other things,
Charley's feeling of being trapped by alien surroundings. The chair
was the riddle that questioned Charley's life.

Rural Arts Exhibition sponsored by Russell Sage Foundation
and U.S. Department of Agriculture, 1937

Jones and I ask the maker's immediate audience about their reactions, but what of the more removed viewer who glimpses folklife in an art gallery? The exhibit of carvings, including chains, is becoming more common, and significant, since galleries usually cater to the elite. At the Seton Hall University Art Gallery in 1983, for instance, a wooden chain lay starkly with the caption "Wooden Chain, 20th century. Artist unidentified. Wood. Length 78 1/2". Private Collection, New Jersey." The catalog announced that "The inclusion of this wooden chain in the exhibition is a deliberate test of the viewer's tolerance for the extremes of what may be called folk art." The viewer was asked to be tolerant, because the curator deemed the chain of "limited invention" and bland ornamentation.[18] From behind the barrier that the pedestal provided, shape, color, and texture—surface messages speaking to cold, aloof evaluation—obscured social symbolism, quieted the maker, and accentuated the dominance of the fine arts and the economic system they represent. The object did not speak for itself, but was made by its new setting to speak the language and reflect the values of urban upper classes. Calling it "art" implied distance in time and place, or that the object lacked use, and had stood still through time. If the curator had called it "crafts," that would have brought the object closer, maybe too close, by implying that the object is not decoration, but labor; not pecuniary, but social; not controlled, but active. Unfamiliar with the social world from whence the object springs, the curator of the art gallery and her viewers reacted superficially to surface design and the patronizing contrast of the deceivingly simple chain to the sterile, normative trappings of the modern world.

Other formats are more populist. County and state fairs often have "handicraft" displays where living rural ingenuity is celebrated. These settings and folk festivals often bring out carved chains to regain a heritage and populist pride. Such, for example, was the intent of the renowned rural handicrafts exhibition put together in 1937 by sociologist Allen Eaton for the U.S. Department of Agriculture and the Russell Sage Foundation.[19] Travelling widely, the show included wooden chains as part of other woodcraft reflecting the integrity and prowess of a rural life threatened or ignored by the growing urban technological society. Aimed primarily at the middle class, this show, and similar ones that followed, used objects and their social background to bemoan disrespect for a subordinate group and warn

Viewers handling a carved fan, East Lansing, Michigan

of the threat to a subculture, perhaps not that far removed, by analogy, to the town and city working class.

I have seen a few persons take no notice of chains or assume that the carver was just "wasting his time." Yet those instances have been rare. With little encouragement, most visitors to my house have zeroed in on my hanging chains, have handled them and have asked me how they are made and why. Free to touch, the viewer handles the object as a technical and intellectual curiosity. The chain is, indeed, riddled with meaning.

The drama between viewer and maker mediated by the object

drew the attention of Nathaniel Hawthrone in his short story, *Drowne's Wooden Image*. Drowne was the woodcarver, and Hawthorne had none other than renowned real-life painter John Singleton Copley looking over Drowne's work. Copley came upon a special object, a half-finished figure, which caused him to exclaim,

"What is here? Who has done this?" he broke out, after contemplating it in speechless astonishment for an instant. "Here is the divine, the life-giving touch. What inspired hand is beckoning this wood to arise and live. Whose work is this?"

"No man's work," replied Drowne. "The figure lies within that block of oak, and it is my business to find it."

"Drowne," said the true artist, grasping the carver fervently by the hand, "You are a man of genius."

Drowne does not think of himself as a man of genius. He is an able man who knows where to cut and smooth. He does not follow the rules of the 'true' artist Copley, but he has the human drive to create and to express. Looking at this figure meant for the ship *Cynosure* (literally, a center of attention), Copley wants Drowne to follow the elite rules of lofty marble statuary, but Drowne insists on his own standards of craftsmanship and compassion.

"Mr. Copley," said Drowne, quietly, "I know nothing of the sculptor's rules of art; but of this wooden image, this work of my hands, this creature of my heart"—and here his voice faltered and choked in a very singular manner—"of this—of her—I may say that I know something."

He knows his craft. He looks for precision and meaning wrought by his own knowledgeable hands. Yet he is the artist still given to inspiration and power. He cannot reach for heights with all his figures, but with some he can feel the excitement of inspired expression. Indeed, Hawthorne writes, "in every human spirit there is imagination, sensibility, creative power, genius, which, according to circumstances, may either be developed in this world or shrouded in a mask of dullness until another state of being."

I sensed Drowne's outlook in the work of George Blume, Floyd Bennington, Wandley Burch, and Earnest Bennett. These are men of skill and compassion; their chains, their cynosures. But they and their audience may deny the full meaning of the work, for its creation and demonstration is sheathed in a ritual of play. George, Floyd, Wandley, and Earnest convey what they do through wood because they have learned their skills informally. Given directly by them to you, the chains and related carvings speak from experience. It comes through in the little rituals attached to introducing and displaying the carvings to viewers and back to the carvers.

"Bet you don't know how I do this," Wandley's introduction, is right, for most do not. How he does it is important, for what it says about the special knowledge he has, and the change of technology around him. And after letting the wood give its lessons to the viewer, the carver can give closing words. Wandley leaves with "Well put it in your pocket if you like it." "Can you appreciate me as Copley would?" he is ever so silently saying. Put the carving close to your heart, and remember the artist who would not be one, the man who knows something special.

THE CARVER'S REPERTOIRE

I didn't meet any carvers who made only chains. Their other carvings varied, but I found recurrent themes and familiar sights when I looked at the other things they had made. The carvers stressed puzzles, playthings, tools, animals, and reminders of rural life. Earnest Bennett arranged his carvings on the table into three sections. On the left he placed replicas of tools and agricultural implements. On the right he put jewelry and bird carvings. Chains and caged balls held center stage. Floyd Bennington had animals and a carved cross surrounding a chain and caged ball that was front and center on a table in the family room. Chains crowded over Wandley Burch's workbench. Behind him sat shelves filled with "crowns of thorns," interlocked pieces of wood forming a hefty wreath, and pairs of small hinged tweezers, "made out of one piece of wood." George Blume's chains loomed over replicas of buildings, tools, animals, and people. The chains pointed the way to related carvings and to other techniques and concerns.

The chain is the keynote of the versatile carver's work. Making the chain initiates the carver. It earns him the right, and gives him the skill, to try other things. Making the chain sets standards of patience and precision. The carver may lay down chain making in favor of other carving, but chain making informs his other whittling. In his popular guidebooks to carving, E.J. Tangerman held up chain carving as an initiation when he wrote, "when the first chain emerges slowly from a block as you watch pop-eyed, particularly if the knife is in your hands, it certainly is 'the thrill that comes once in a lifetime.' " "Difficult and tricky to make," according to Tangerman, the chain and caged ball have always been a whittler's standard.[20] Making the chain is analogous to the all-important "jazz standard" in music, a tune every jazz musician worthy of the title knows and improvises. Building on the basic theme, the carver can set down links of different sizes and shapes, and make different combinations of chain and caged balls. The chain is at once the most varied and most repeated of the carver's repertoire.

If the carver makes a chain and caged ball, chances are that he knows other puzzles from the whittler's bag of tricks. Pliers, fans, and block puzzles fall into this category. Making pliers in wood plays on cutting in a hinge joint that allows the normally immovable wood to swivel freely. Having cut in a hinge joint with the sharp tip of the pocketknife, the carver can shape the rest of the wood into pliers, tweezers, shears, and scissors. And again he can brag, "all made out of just one piece of wood with nothing but my pocketknife." Wandley Burch also adds a boast of time, saying he can produce a tweezer in two minutes. The skeptical child is delighted when he turns a bland stick that might have been thrown away into a hinged play tool. Earnest Bennett elaborates upon the tweezer by making one out of a toothpick. George Blume drew attention to his pliers using the hinged joint by the rich detail he carved in to make it look like the "real thing."

A variation of making a mechanical joint in wood is to make a pivot joint allowing the wood to swivel. Using this technique can result in making swivelling razors, locks, wrenches, knives, doors that swing, and even a bicycle. As with the caged ball, the trick is to cut everywhere but where the ball or pivot is to be. Our tendency is to think that objects are cut *out*, but in making balls, hinges, or pivots out of one piece of wood, the object is cut *in*. Some of that tendency, carvers will occasionally tell you, is found in society. "Cut something out, before you try to work with what you got, they say, but an old country boy never throws anything out you know," Wandley Burch

Pliers made by Earnest Bennett

told me. In making these trick tools, the carver fools your natural
assumption of how to proceed, and forces you to think again, about
his technique and maybe about him.

Making a pivot in a carved wooden pocketknife is a favorite of
carvers, because it enshrines in precious wood the extension of the
carver's hand. Wandley Burch made his more realistic by putting in
a wooden backspring. Earnest Bennett gave his an extra touch, too,
by using wood that made it look old-timey. Earnest also used several
pivots to make an old-style bicycle. Using the pivot joint, George
Blume made an old straight razor in wood that he adored. It had
several blades attached and folded into a case. The carvers also gave
the special treatment of wood to other old-time tools, such as the
versatile draw knife and common buck saw. Another popular one was
the *Schnitzelbank*, as the German carvers called it, or the "shaving
horse," a bench used for making shingles and planing wood with a
draw knife. George Blume and Wandley Burch were also proud of

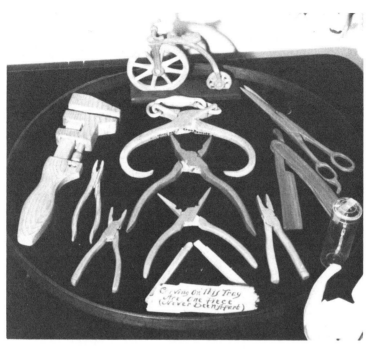

Above, Earnest's razor, scissors, pliers, wrench, and bicycle.
Below, Wandley's two-in-one pliers.

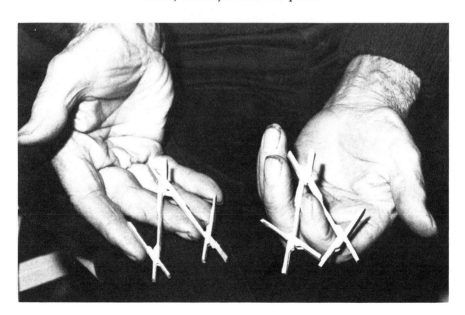

wooden replicas of broad axes they made. They held these wooden treasures like scepters, symbols of ceremony and authority marking a man's status.

Fans and birds with "fan-tails" are also common among the carvers. George made a peacock that had a fan unfold behind the bird. Earnest Bennett made a fan with a fancy handle. The trick here is to slice the wood out of a block so that the wood strips can be bent out and interlocked. Again, the carvers boast of making the fan out of one piece of wood. Wandley Burch's crown of thorns is not from one piece, but it relies on the powerful visual effect of interlocking wood. He cuts flat arrow-shaped pieces of wood with spaces in them to interlock. After interlocking about fifty such pieces he takes a tiny peg and clamps the last two pieces to form a circle. The shape that emerges is a wreath. These are popular in Scandinavia now as Christmas decorations; in America carvers present them as tricks, for the wreath can be bent inside out and still retain its shape.

Pieces for Wandley's crown of thorns

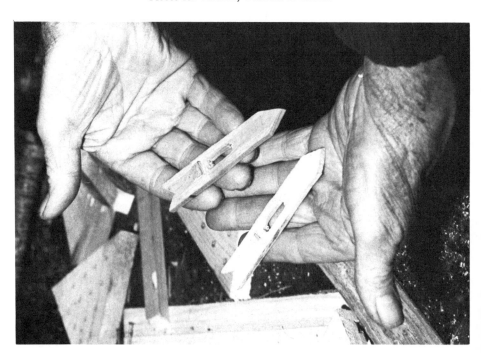

Above, wooden wreath made in Denmark, 1977. Below, Wandley's crown of thorns.

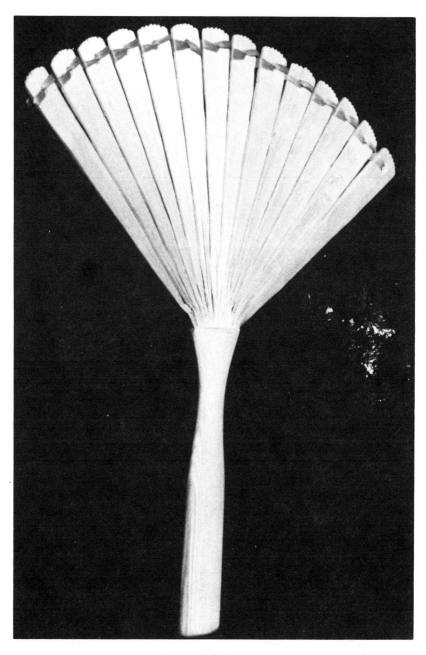

Fan made by Earnest

Six-stick puzzle made by Willie Hausmann

There is more to the whittler's store of puzzles. The whittler takes apart a wooden cube made out of four or more pieces and invites the viewer to put it back together. Long before Rubik's cube came along, these puzzles, found in the various shapes of, for example, a barrel, egg, or hexagon, had solution seekers wringing and twisting their hands around the apparently simple puzzle. Not only do the wooden puzzles test the ability to put them together, but taking them apart can often be as elusive! And if that isn't enough to bring forth a few muttered curses, Wandley Burch has ox-yoke puzzles. A wooden bar has two loops of string hanging from it. A wooden disk is strung through each loop. The challenge is to put both disks on one loop and then get it back to the way it was. The result is usually a tangled mess, unless the person thinks of pulling the string through the bar.

Other puzzles don't have logical solutions but trick the viewer into thinking that there might be. The "idiot stick" is a prime example. Wandley Burch would hand a two-inch, round piece of wood with a tip to an unsuspecting person. He would show a rubber band through the two-inch section, and then pull the tip out of the section to reveal a notch in a shaft that runs from the tip into the two-inch section. He would tell the person that he has to hook the notch into the rubber band so that it snaps shut. The person tries and tries to no avail. That is because he was deceived, for Wandley did not hook the notch but used his thumb and forefinger to snap the tip into the section. The hand is indeed faster than the eye.

Deceiving logic is also the name of the game when a viewer is shown an arrow through a target. A wooden arrow appears stuck in a disk, but how did it get in there? There is no evidence of a break in the disk through which would the carver would have put the arrow. The answer is again that the carver started with a solid block of wood and cut the arrow in. The carver has made a three-dimensional optical illusion according to his own brand of hewn logic.

Earnest Bennett and Wandley Burch liked to make puzzles and playthings for children. Puzzles delighted and, the carvers thought, taught the children. Just for play were Earnest's whimmy-diddles and old-time spinning tops. Wandley made little figures, windmills, and rattles, which were multiple balls in cages. Other objects were made for adults. Wandley had a "man in a barrel," for example. When he

Floyd's pig and trough

Horse and chain made by Linus Herbig

pushed down the top of the man, a tiny stick would pop up where his genitals would be. Of course many of the children's things also fascinated the adults, especially the block puzzles.

Reminders of rural life were the most common accompaniment to carvers' chains. You could usually expect to see a carving of a farmhouse or of furniture. George Blume prolifically made log houses and barns remembered from his Siberia, Indiana, childhood. In Wandley's kitchen, a photograph of his old farmstead stood over carvings of an old farmhouse and barn. Floyd Bennington made furniture, the nostalgic rocker and liar's bench. Floyd also specializes in incredibly detailed animals. He spent months working on a pig feeding out of a trough which he gave to Lil Blemker as a present. The carved animals were either of farm animals or of pets like cats and dogs. Earnest Bennett was also adept at bird carvings, recalling home decoy carving.

Just as the carver develops and displays his skill by creating many objects of different sorts, the carvings themselves encourage viewers to expand their thinking and senses, especially that of touch. And they bring the viewer "in touch" with the memories and realities of the carvers, and some of the illusions of society.

CHAPTER THREE

How Do You Figure It, That Darn Stuff?

MIDNIGHT passed. Geogre Blume's basement kept out the night air. Sawdust filled his nostrils as he sat at his basement workbench. In the morning, he would go to the factory. He didn't have that many more days of work there before retirement, that many more days of making furniture for unseen customers.

But now he carved for himself. The only sounds were the scraping and cutting of his tools and an occasional word from George about his nascent carving.

"I'll carve until I'm ready for bed," he thought. "It shouldn't be long."

He looked up at his wooden progeny. Chains draped over shelves. Some were supposed to be watch chains, others trace and log chains. The wooden handcuffs attached to chains caught his eye. "Now ain't they somethin'?" he thought. Over in the corner, "Home Sweet Home" cut in wood sat idly as time passed. Unlike at the factory, it was the task, not the time, that mattered here.

"Aaah," he let out, holding a few more links in his hand. He felt pleased and hardly tired until he thought about it.

He checked his watch. Could it be? He read five in the morning. "I must have lost all track of time," he said to himself. He still felt driven. He picked up his chain and held it closely.

When he showed one to fellow workers, they thought it a puzzle, but now his making of it puzzled him. He wasn't sure why he did it, only that it was important to him.

Years later he still wondered. He had some ideas, but he was bewildered by what he had accomplished and what drove him to it. All those hours, all those carvings swept through his mind, for now he couldn't carve. His hands and eyes failed him. He missed it sorely.

"How do you figure it, that darn stuff?" he poignantly asked me.

Many men in southern Indiana, indeed across America and beyond, carve chains and similarly puzzling objects. In this chapter I summarize my interpretations of those objects, and the men who make them, so that I can answer George's striking question.

Chain carving is at first glance compelling because of the dangling links that the carver freely releases, again and again, from a solid block of wood, usually with only the aid of a pocketknife. The wooden chain presents a visual riddle, challenging you to propose principles that would explain an apparently illogical construction. But why do these men whom I met, mostly elderly and with rural backgrounds, make objects that require so much time and seem to serve so little apparent purpose? Carving often was a way for these men to adjust to a new or distressing situation. For those who really took to it, chain carving helped clarify their identites and reduce their anxieties.

The men I interviewed were all active chain carvers at the time, and most continue to carve to this day. Chain carving's ancient and global tradition did not concern these men as much as their perception of the way chain carving fit into their lives. Chain carving embodied values and skills from a rural way of life characteristic of America's "wooden age." Now surrounded by a different reality, carving reminded them where they've been and who they are.

Although carvers often mentioned "meeting the challenge" and "passing the time" as their reasons for carving chains, they had deeper motives. To be sure, passing the time was important for these elderly men because of stretches of enforced idleness and loneliness in their lives. Yet they still felt useful and productive, and they were able to show that through carving.

"I passed many a happy hour," George Blume explained, "where otherwise I might have been sitting there worrying about this and about that. Chain carving takes your time up, see, get your mind off it—take the worrying away from me." Floyd Bennington agreed. "I've heard it said lots of times; there's something about carving a piece of wood that you have in your hand—it quiets your nerves—just to keep your mind off something else."

Carving especially came into use during crises, when the carvers had to adjust to abrupt changes. The word "chain" sounds like "change," and probably invokes subconsciously the effects of life's changes. Floyd Bennington's retirement, by his own admission, troubled him. He had played a central role in his community, and he was unprepared for the alienation that retirement brought. For him, chain carving was a way to stay productive and to displace thoughts of the frailty of advancing age.

Willie Hausmann in St. Philip, Indiana, started carving chains in reaction to his wife's sudden death. It helped him adjust to the loneliness. It soothed him to grasp and stroke the wood and to release objects from the solid block. People usually regard touching and rubbing as soothing emotionally, and the stress on these actions in chain carving helps carvers cope with the loss of a loved one who gave caressing.

Chain carving cannot only *remind* one of change but can also *bring* change. It draws a carver closer to others. Carvers show or give their carvings to people in their community or family. I think of George making a special chain for his daughter or Wandley Burch making chains for his grandchildren. Earnest Bennett's wife proudly shows off a wooden chain bracelet he made with a linked heart at the end. A carver of wooden pliers, Leo Klueh, told me he gave his dentist a carving to show him the little extra feeling that money lacks.

One shouldn't discount the inner, personal satisfaction that carving can give. As Floyd once said, "It's a *can you do it* thing." To hold up a difficult and tricky carving born out of your own hands produces an excitement of accomplishment, of bringing talent out from within. Chain carving keeps the mind and body active when the need to do so is strong but the means may not always be evident, as in old age. It can build pride and confidence.

Chain carving helps establish personal space and time. Floyd Bennington gave up many activities because he had to care for his invalid wife. Maintaining his carving allowed him time to escape to his workshop—his individual, masculine space—and to preserve his personal identity. He could still have a sense of self.

George Blume admittedly did not get along with his wife, but his orthodox Catholicism prevented him from obtaining a divorce. His basement workshop became his own small, private world filled with carvings of familiar old buildings, vehicles, implements, animals, people, and activities—and many chains, locks, pliers, and caged balls. After he moved to his daughter's house and the carvings had been gone for years he reflected, "I just get homesick for that stuff. I go to bed sometimes thinking about that stuff. That was nothing ordinary. That was something strange, something extraordinary." His choice of words is noteworthy, for homesick connotes the home within a home he created, his self-identity within another identity. His emphasis on extraordinary underscores how his carvings transcended the ordinary time and place which troubled him. He could create a situation in which he felt more comfortable mentally and emotionally. As for his use of the word *strange*, the out-of-the ordinary can dramatize and exaggerate the problems one has. It draws attention to itself and to oneself.

Many carvers told me of their fears of approaching death. How did carving fit in? Alois Schuch, a Jasper, Indiana, woodcarver, rhetorically explained. "I would die just sitting here if I didn't carve and then what would be left of me?" He carved old-time furniture, agricultural implements, playthings, and, yes, chains.[1] I also think of Leonard Langebrake, a cane carver and rug weaver from Huntingburg. I sat on Leonard's porch asking him about his life of craft. He put a handcarved cane of his in my hand. "Take that. I'll be dead soon and then you'll know what that cane means and where it's from." Two weeks later he died. But he left the world knowing his objects would endure.

By making chains and other folk forms, and by showing their knowledge to younger generations, old carvers feel that they will be remembered after death as practitioners of a custom that represents traditional, often rural, values. Frequently, the carvers feel that such values need reinforcement, especially in the industrial milieu of their elderly years. Carvers often learned from an elderly neighbor or family member, and they in turn try to bridge the generations. As children, they were trained to assume skills they would need later as men. They learned the proper masculine use of tools, became familiar with work and production outside the woman's domain (to their way of thinking, the home), and learned about the outdoors and the preciousness of woods. Late in their lives, carving reminded them of their young experience and let others know its value.

By having the special knowledge of making chains, carver's imagine that they increase their status, for the wooden chain, being a

Matchstick chain by Earnest Bennett

technical and perceptual puzzle, displays a carver's exceptional skill, patience, and creativity. As Floyd Bennington remarked, "If it's something that's out of the ordinary, it attracts lots of attention. Oh yes, I feel better when somebody comes along with 'I don't see how you did it.' " With the unusual chain, the carver still retains power.

Several carvers—George Blume, Linus Herbig, and Alios Schuch, to name a few—worked in furniture factories in Huntingburg and Jasper. They often had specialized tasks on an assembly line, which reduced the pride achieved from completing a whole piece of furniture by themselves. Making creative objects like chains provided them a means of impressing their peers with their woodworking skills. They demonstrated a command of the wood and a pride in their ability by making a traditional woodcarver's object "all by myself." To add an ironic twist, they consistently used scrap wood from the furniture they were employed to make. It reminds me of photocopy machines being used to reproduce office broadsides that ridicule the very technology that makes it possible.[2] Coal miners in Pennsylvania, for example, would carve figures on their own time out of loose coal left about. Creativity provided a break in the routine of industrial work, lifting the mind above the job's lack of creativity. Carvings, whether wood or coal, can be seen as attempts to insert an element of humanness into the work experience and to provide an outlet for tension.

The carver controls all the steps of creation, from choosing the piece of wood to the final polishing of the newly created object's surface. He does not work for anyone else; the carving belongs to him totally; it signifies wholeness. Showing the chain to a viewer is the culmination of a technical process, for the chain's appearance implies that the carver did it all. This is a manifestation of the craftsman ideal, which we admire, and it signifies an older, traditional way of doing things. Hence, the carver attracts respect and appreciation. Carving sets him apart, giving him attention and identity.

In the playful drama that takes place between the creator and the viewer, the viewer not only looks at the object, he touches and handles it. An air of play attached to showing the chain conceals some of the deeper messages the chain holds, even as it gives abstract clues to them and allows the viewer to get closer to the object and maker. In imposing literally a "first-hand" experience on the object, the viewer also imposes a reality on its maker. Up to this point, the chain has been handled only by the carver. Now he chooses to share it with the viewer. There is some loss of control and hence some apprehension. By taking the chain and handling it, the viewer affirms, "Things are well in hand!"

Since chains and similar objects show the carver's skill and creativity, many carvers use chains to relate socially to people, although their actual carving is typically a solitary task. For instance, carvers commonly offer their objects as friendship and love tokens. Rarely, if at all, do they sell their work. Wandley Burch and Willie Hausmann made chains for their grandchildren and other friends and family, reinforcing the ties between giver and recipient. Giving away their carvings reminded them of where and with whom they belonged. It reminded them, occasionally, of men in their childhoods who gathered with their whittling in public places like the courthouse square or the general store. They gave their whittling, if it looked good, to a smiling child or old friend. Chains were social tools. They were the ties that bind, the carver's behavioral links to social and personal identity.

The wooden chain's boast of handwork and the use of the pocket-knife betoken skills and activities common to many carvers' childhoods. Many of the carvers resumed carving in old age after a hiatus in middle age, partly to remind them of their earlier lives. Working with the wood made them feel closer to nature and in control of a product. Carvers viewed whittling as a reaction to the modern technological era—an era which removes, in their eyes, an object's means of production from worker and consumer and which is at odds with nature.

For audiences, chain carving is a "craft," and thus harks back to an earlier time. Festivals and community groups ask carvers like Earnest Bennett and Wandley Burch to demonstrate their skill as something reminiscent of pioneer days. Even though chain carving is widespread and very much alive today, it is presented to audiences as a reminder of the past. This was also the case earlier, too. In the 1930s, collector Allen Eaton, working with the Russell Sage Foundation, equated folk carving with "a long-established mode of living not concerned with urban schedules."[3] Visitors to the 1981 Festival of American Folklife in Washington, D.C., were told, "We like to think that folk crafts harken back to an earlier, simpler time—an era of small town insularity before the intrusion of machine-manufactured goods and other commonplaces of the industrial age."[4] Therein is found the social vision of craft today. It has become an acting out of older values and skills, a balance to technological change. Yet dictionaries and objective observation define *craft* as handwork, in which terms new skills emerge daily, from a child's paperfolding to a sheetmetal worker's impromptu sculpting with scrap materials. These do not generally enter crafts festivals, however, for they do not fulfill a social need to shape a category to act as a vantage for looking back.

From the safe haven of the past, symbols emerge. Because craft is not part of the machinery that runs daily life, the craftsman is free to be abstract. He is himself an abstraction of work, or what work once was, and because the things he makes are free of utility, they can take on many dimensions of meaning. Open to interpretation, the things he makes decorate and challenge, surprise and puzzle. The craftsman embodies the human capacity to preserve older values, such as the use of one's hands to make things. Objects made in such a way

Earnest's endless chain

carry an element of compassion in them that ordinary, machine-made objects lack. The chain carver, especially, is charged with making symbols of human qualities.

The chain as a love and friendship token relies on the symbol of linking, a common image of love and marriage. The "endless chain" is a special variation of the chain symbolizing continuity and permanence. The endless chain is a closed loop instead of the usual rectilinear chain. Its unusual loop adds an extra magic to its appearance. Steve Snoish, a priest from Evansville, Indiana, makes interlocking hearts. People use these socially accepted symbols to reinforce in material form, as a chain would, an abstract relationship. In effect, words may not be able to express how a person feels about another, but an object like a chain can.

Symbolism also exists that is outside awareness. Chains can dramatize feelings of imprisonment, restriction, and containment. Wooden chains, cages, pliers, hooks, and locks may be unconscious,

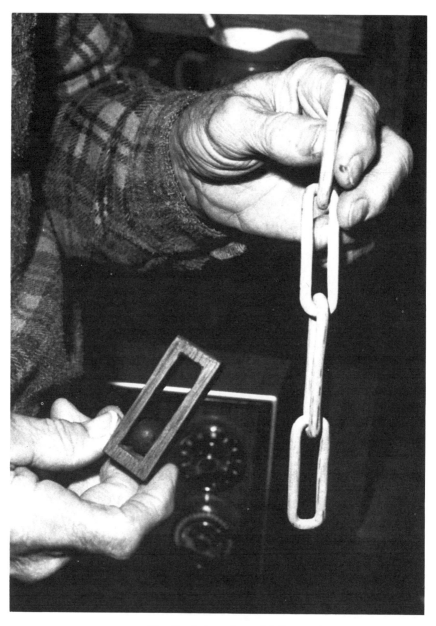

Floyd's chain and caged ball

but not coincidental, symbols for the carvers. Such objects are often projections of carvers' mental conflicts or uncertainties. The common addition to the chain of a caged ball gives a ball, a chain, and a cage—all symbols of imprisonment. The behavioral restrictions a carver feels as a result of his anxieties or fears may be symbolized in the restrictive chain and in the structured procedure of chain carving. At the same time, the "release" of chain carving compensates for the restrictions. Indeed, when I asked Wandley Burch how he chose the times he would carve, he replied, "When I feel chained, I make chains; when I feel caged, I make cages."

The chain's connectivity represents continuity, the opposite of disruption produced by conflict. Chain carving symbolizes freedom of choice within a set structure. Carving "in" the ball, pivot, and hinge, rather than "cutting out," is a statement, too, about alienation. The audience is deluded by the chain and caged ball, because they expect the object to be cut out. But the carver has cut the object in, much as he wants to cut himself in. He shows himself and the audience that cutting him out, because of his age and outmoded skill, is not the answer. He has skills that the uninitiated cannot grasp.

Wooden chains and their carving can have opposite symbols working—continuity and disruption, alienation and integration. Carving itself is ambiguous, for it is done alone, for oneself, yet shared with others. Wooden chains and their carving can be simultaneously a symptom of a carver's anxieties and a compensation for those anxieties. A symbolic ambivalence is often expressed, for the object can evoke simultaneous responses of freedom and restriction, pleasure and pain. That very ambiguity is life, as Floyd Bennington liked to say, and that ambiguity, that life-force, gives the chain its expressive power, its affecting presence.

But why would the symbolism rest in chains and cages? Floyd Bennington mentioned that he felt like a prisoner in his own house, because of the restriction forced on him by the needs of his invalid wife. George Blume confined himself to his basement, a conscious choice to avoid the pain of his marriage. Chains and cages encapsulated their hidden feelings, yet could be presented publicly with a smile.

Carvers often talked metaphorically about *releasing* or *freeing* connected links from a solid *block* of wood. They recognized, however, that forces, stresses, and tensions exist that can drive the links *apart.* Normally they don't want to glue the breaks and cracks together artificially and temporarily. The connectivity of the links is, indeed, an illusion, for the wood (like a person) is considered fragile and prone to breaking and cracking. Another indication of chains as a projection of anxieties is a typical pose assumed by carvers when I photographed them with their chains. Many carvers spontaneously put their chains around their necks and bodies, symbolic of confinement.

By symbolizing conflicts in material form the carver excludes painful impulses from his mind by redirecting his inner feelings toward an external form. The difficulties of industrial life, old age, retirement, impotence, illness, loneliness, and death produce anxieties. The topics recurred often when carvers talked about their lives. Several people pointed to a direct connection between chain carving and a time in life particularly marked by anxiety. Floyd Bennington's wife, for example, told me, "I couldn't understand how he could whittle, being so nervous after he quit teaching, but he told me it was relaxing." When questioned about his motives for chain carving, Floyd replied, "It took away my tension, got my mind off my retirement." Several years later he reflected on a different use of chain carving: "It helped me get over the bad times when my wife got sick."

The use of creativity to deal with anxiety is not unusual, but if creativity requires thought, sweat, and endurance, why would people voluntarily want to make things? Psychotherapist Anthony Storr explains that people use creative activity as a veiled defense. The human ego, he says, "is vulnerable to anxiety against which, since anxiety is unpleasant, it attempts to defend itself."[5] Creativity celebrates a person's ego. It exercises control and power. It emphasizes wholeness.

At the same time, creativity can imply separateness. When being creative, one often feels that one is doing something different or discovering something new. Carl Rogers, in proposing a theory of creativity, described this anxiety of separateness as a concomitant to the desire to communicate. "It is doubtful," he says, "whether a human being can create, without wishing to share his creation. It is the only way he can assuage the anxiety of separateness and assure himself that he belongs to the group."[6] Chain carvers, as retired, older men, feel separate from society, and the act of carving itself is at odds with an industrialized society. But in sharing the finished chain with others they effect a reintegration with society, they connect with others. The chain's combination of artificial shapes like rectangles and natural shapes like curves in one chain also calls for integration, yet can emphasize the separateness of motifs such as caged balls or imply tension that exists between trapped ball, imprisoning cage, and mediating links.

Creativity can help alleviate mental distress, but not all activity indulged in for this purpose is creative. Storr mentions the man who takes his car on the highway, "not because he wants to get anywhere, but because he wants to get away from himself, a manoeuvre facilitated by fast driving since this requires a high degree of concentration on the external world."[7] Some activities pursued for emotional reasons reflect different degrees of creativity. I know of friends who bake bread when they are down. The find a release in the preparation and completion of a handmade product. They enjoy the kneading and pounding, which helps them emotionally. They find aesthetic satisfaction in playing with and perfecting the texture, color, and shape of the loaf. Although following a recipe, they take pride in "doing it themselves." They may very well give a loaf away and wait for words of praise, or with family or friends may "break bread together," becoming just a little closer.

Woodcarvings have the advantage of enduring. The carver, like the baker, collects tools and materials and makes the object by hand. The wood allows him to cut, scrape, and file a design out of natural substances. More so than the baker, he manipulates and perfects the texture, color, and design to his own liking, and later he may share his creation with others. He feels renewed.

Carvings are products of imagination which can allow the carver to escape into a world of his own making—often a fantasy world. The artistic creation of an imaginary or fantastic thing is a common human mechanism for dealing with troubles or conflicts. From Charley's "strange" rocking chair to Sam Rodia's "mysterious" Watts Towers, the sense is one of shutting out the external world and building the internal world of the self. The imagination lets an anxious person escape disturbing realities for an environment where the maker is in control of order and events.

George Blume escaped into the unreal world of his basement, filled with his fantastic carvings. After almost fifteen years he had completed almost a thousand carvings—many of buildings, tools, and characters remembered from his childhood—in addition to twenty long chains strewn across the room. His activity formed a "mental block," another common reaction to anxiety, whereby a person pursues an activity that demands concentration on itself rather than on the problems in his life. Indeed, the carvers easily admitted that carving got their "minds off" what troubled them. It was no coincidence, I believe, that most chain carvers I met were old and anxious about being old, idle, and alienated from modern technological life. Their remove from mainstream society in part motivated them to take up a traditional, relaxing practice that reassured them.

Motivation is one thing, compulsion another. George Blume's late night carving, which opened this chapter, is an example of a compulsive drive to make things. What is it about people that drives them to work past their bodies' normal tolerance? Storr argued that creative activity, when used excessively by some people as a defense against mental distress, amounts to an addiction. "Such individuals pursue their creative endeavour so relentlessly that they are never able to take a holiday from their work, and feel miserable or ill if they cannot engage in it. Just as a diabetic deprived of insulin will become ill, so a creative person deprived of his work may become mentally disturbed."[8] In cases like this, outside recognition isn't necessary. The mental benefits can be enough, but that doesn't really explain some carvers' feelings of being driven.

Storr was not far off the mark, however, when he used the metaphor of injection. There are similarities between injection, especially as a response to emotional withdrawal, and the carving done by the old men. The men reported feeling withdrawn, sometimes depressed, and often insecure. Carving, like injection, is a repeated activity that gives quick results, which in turn encourage further repetition. Chain carving, especially, is a sustained, open-ended activity, because the chain extends as far as the carver wants to take it. The effect can be hypnotic. The carver *gives* himself the effect— controls the "injection," if you will—because he chooses how often and how long he will carve. Experiments, including several by John R. Nichols, have shown that subjects administering drugs to themselves, rather than passively receiving them, were more likely to be addicted.[9] Self-directed activity increases the strength of habit.

Also recalling the thrust of an injection are activities that require piercing, cutting, and penetrating. Carving, with its symbolic cutting and piercing, reduces the withdrawal distress of the men I met. It's a release, much as breaking through a paper hoop at a football game, cutting through red tape, or making a stab is. The carver's knife injects changes into the wood, having been preceded by changes in concepts in the carver's mind. Rather than being "sustained opiate-directed behavior," as Nichols called addictive behavior caused by self-administered drug injection, carving, for George at least, became "sustained creative-directed behavior." Often what he made was less important to him than the making of it. He wanted to experience the sensation of cutting and controlling. The image of change in the wood before him, and the change that he imagined around him, kept him going. He stopped his carving years later when it began tormenting him, reminding him of his frailty rather than his control. Still, it was not a habit easily abandoned. He did, as he said, get homesick for the carving. He didn't always know what drove him so, but in carving he found an activity worth repeating, for it brought him into the web of his mind and body, nature and culture, past and present.

The elderly often revive practices remembered from childhood. The pattern is known as a "regression-progression behavioral complex"—a mouthful of a label but useful in describing what is going on. When a carver resumes chain carving in old age after a long hiatus, he reactivates conduct that in earlier and supposedly simpler stages of his development helped him adjust. Faced with adjustments to old age, retirement, death, or an alien industrial or urban environment, the carver nostalgically revives a creative behavior which helped him adjust as a child to adulthood. The repetition and predictability of making the traditional form eases fears of the unpredictable or threatening situation. That is the "regression" part. The "progression" part comes in because the carver feels renewed and alive with the sense of discovery. The carver's mind is uplifted by taking on a new challenge, setting a goal, and experiencing the thrill of innovative, creative activity.

A carver does not necessarily need a crisis to begin carving, but certain crises were mentioned by carvers—alienation from society and family, lack of productivity, frailty, illness, loneliness, fear of death—their friends' and loved ones' and their own. The only carver to mention a sexual crisis, however, was George Blume, who spoke of "your dick not getting hard no more." Although not often talked about, the prospect of impotence with advancing age is a common anxiety, especially among old men. It is conceivable that the caged balls and chains-on-shafts symbolize sexual restriction or impotence. Notably, men have traditionally made such objects for women, usually their sexual partners. Men in England, in fact, made wooden knitting sheaths with balls, usually two, in cages with attached chains, and called them "pricks."[10] The number of balls carved into other love tokens were said to represent the number of children conceived or desired.[11] In America and Wales, wooden chains are frequently attached to spoons, and spooning is a slang term for courting or sexual intercourse, based on the metaphorical "fit" of overlapping spoons.[12] Wandley Burch did talk about being "down in the hole," his phrase for his womblike workshop. He was also fascinated, he told me, by his ability in chain carving to "make a piece of wood longer than its original size." But while the fact remains that chain carving embodies sexual connotations and some terms used to discuss it also have sexual connotations, an interpretation based on such symbolism is, I think, stretching the point. The coincidence of sexual anxiety and the sexual symbolism of the chain may have significance to some, but not all, carvers.

Other insecurities and uncertainties were mentioned more by the carvers, and found symbolic expression in chain carving. Old age need not be a bleak time, but its approach does often raise serious fears. When contrasted with youth, by youth, old age might appear worse than it is, because loss is emphasized. But George Blume, Wandley Burch, Floyd Bennington, and Earnest Bennett, discovered through their carving the gains of aging. They used their extra time to their advantage; they built a tangible self. Barbara Myerhoff, an anthropologist, has called this an attitude toward aging as a career. The members of a senior center she studied, like the men I met, "had provided themselves with new possiblities to replace those that had been lost, regularly set new standards for themselves in terms of which to measure growth and achievement, sought and found meaning in their lives, in the short run and the long."[13] Carving was not just an attempt to get up from a bed of sorrows, but indeed, dressing up the bed of years. The men brought to their carving standards of work, values of living, and demands for success that they had before retirement. Carving, with its tendency for encapsulating varied symbolism, had a double-edged appeal. I thought of that especially when I saw a carving special to George Blume but also found among other carvers. It was a straight razor that was lifelike down to the last detail, save two: it was in wood, and it had two blade edges. "That'll fool ya," George said. It was another riddle of real and unreal brought together. One edge was reality, and the other the carver's imagination, which could also cut through the tangles of life. Carving celebrated the continuity of the values and standards of the carver and also points to new needs and demands.

The carver didn't always search the psyche for symbolism. Sometimes it was enough to play with forms, putting them together in new combinations. The carver used shapes and textures to have designs dance for his eyes. The child piling rocks or the old man whittling down a stick feels a charge, because they are arranging, changing, and playing. "Art for its own sake?" To be sure, each person reacts differently to any particular anxiety, or one may indeed not be directly motivated by conflict. Creatively working with aesthetically pleasing forms as an end in itself is a common motive.[14] Assuming for the moment, however, that a conflict exists in the mind of the carver at a given time, he may unconsciously continue to use carving as a defense even at a time when no conflict, or indeed reason for celebration, exists, because of the original reinforcement which he experienced from carving. He can use carving for different purposes. Floyd Bennington first revived his chain carving for the challenge, and then did it more actively in his retirement. Carving does not go on unwittingly, as some observers would assume. Whether to play with forms or deal unconsciously with anxiety, carving is motivated, and in the case of George Blume, highly driven. To know those motives and the conditions surrounding them is to know how creativity becomes action.

Chain carving is part of a range of human behaviors people use to express creativity, and therefore chains are not some freakish class of objects. People have different talents and traditions that they enact in selective situations, depending on their assessment of needs and desires. Because creativity suggests problems to solve, one sometimes makes things to *find* meaning, not just deliver it. A solution in wood may offer a solution in mind. When a person's choice of an outlet for ambiguities and uncertainties becomes perfected, the product may be perceived as "art" or "craft." Having mastered the skill, he carries over his confidence to other areas of life in an effort to work out uncertainties or troubles. For some people, of course, carving a chain can actually increase anxiety (as it did for me!), but for the men I met, chain carving was especially appropriate to them and their families. It was a familiar skill at which they excelled and in which they therefore conveyed their feelings.

Creativity is expressive; it is symbolic. The carver cannot always control the meanings he conveys. He finishes the carving often with only a bare notion of why it is important. Nonetheless, the carving speaks in a silent, yet profound, symbolic language. The person who receives the chain may not always be aware of its full meaning but he may very well feel its influence. The viewer often stops at the surface messages of play and whimsy, but deeper symbols lie within the object. The surface can, sometimes, direct you to the object's depth. By presenting the chain to you, the carver makes you use your hands. You touch it, trying to figure it out. At that moment you are in his way of thinking. You are using your hands, the hallmark of his craft and life, to solve a problem. You are taking his standpoint, and you are learning something about being a craftsman, for you sympathize with his feelings and you attach a connection to the object that probably did not exist before. That's one way the symbols are conveyed, by bringing the viewer into the carver's frame of thinking. The carver himself relies on symbols that are shaped by his experience and belief. The wood, the knife, the chain, and the neighborliness of giving the object come from his background.

Another way the symbols are conveyed is by their spontaneous associations. Whether young or old, the person looking at the chain connects those forms with common symbolism. The chain brings to mind the uses of chains as links, as barriers, as tools. The craft it shows brings the past into the present.

Still another way the symbols are effectively conveyed is through the tensions that exist in the carved chain. The chain is real and unreal. It is continuous and disruptive, part of nature and part of culture. By containing these opposing traits, the chain is ambiguous. It builds up a tension between its parts that heightens its overall effect, because it forces you to take notice. Think of the contradition of the thorny crown, the do-nothing machine, and, of course, the wooden chain. You think them unusual because of that blurring of categories. You wonder what is going on. You look closer and run through the object's parts in your head. The ambiguous object stands taut in your mind. You often find yourself grasping at dimensions other than what you see in front of you. The object points you toward the complexity of meaning.

We are all creative in our own ways. George, Floyd, Wandley, and Earnest thought of woodcarving as part of who they were, even though they didn't always do it in the past. Persons commonly turn to what they think they do well and creatively, in reaction to pressures on their lives. They might bake bread, shoot a basketball, or play a song, but the underlying creative mechanisms and aesthetic principles work similarly. It is that human drive for control and connection, form and feeling, beauty and expression, that culminates in creativity.

Chain carving exhibits special characteristics of folk design. Its skill is learned informally, its design both repeats and varies, and its normal context is outside the official "art world." The carving is made with local materials and is locally distributed. It fits in with traditional ideas about how crafty things are done and arranged. Folk design stresses customary forms and familiar practices even as it commands variation. Its rules are structured, but informally, so that plenty leeway is allowed, and desired, for personal whim. Just as the creative urge behind chain carving gives it an extra dimension, so, too, does its folkness. It connects the carver and his designs socially and culturally to firm roots, to where he feels comfortable. It ties him, or so he thinks, to "tradition," thus lending a flexible regularity and predictability to his life.

To simply label it *folk* could be misleading though, if that means relegating it to some subclass of creativity. Chain carving shares attributes of most creativity: it involves aesthetic judgment; it requires skill and a sense of form; and it results in products of noticeable and often pleasing arrangements. The products commonly have various levels of meaning. The realization that an artificial hierarchy is commonly imposed on creativity of a traditional nature led Michael Owen Jones to end his study of a most expressive Kentucky chairmaker with the assertion, "There is, indeed, only one art, not two or three or four, and it is to be found universally in human experience as an integral, not isolable, element of man's behavior."[15] What changes is the context that identifies and frames the behavior, whether an "art world" or holler, a gallery or factory. Our attitude toward creative expression is influenced by our social surroundings and our values gained in youth, our particular perception of what is evocative and worthy, and what is common and practical out of which creativity arises— but the impulse to create remains constant.

"How do you figure it, that darn stuff?" It made George and others feel good, but they usually weren't sure why. They did it consistently at idle or stressful times in their lives. The chains' enigmatic, aesthetic characteristics and the symbols the chain suggests gives it a powerful appeal to carvers and viewers. It can be an instrument of adjustment and play, a token of identity and expression, an object of tradition, of self and society.

Chain carving is full of meaning for carvers and their audiences. Meaning—knowing where you belong, who you are, and what you know and do is consequential—is etched in the things people make. However humbly and subtly, chain carvers teach how humans shape meaning and value from the world, and how they carve it into their lives.

George could be the cane carver in the parable given by Henry David Thoreau in *Walden*. Thoreau's carver made a staff, and kept perfecting it, even as his home city changed with time. "As he made no compromise with Time, Time kept out of his way, and only sighed at a distance because he could not overcome him." This man, this artist seeking perfection in wood, "had made a new system in making a staff, a world with full and fair proportions. . . . And now he saw by the heap of shavings still fresh at his feet, that, for him and his work, the former lapse of time had been an illusion, and that no more time had elapsed than is required for a single scintillation from the brain of Brahma to fall on and inflame the tinder of a mortal brain. The material was pure, and his art was pure; how could the result be other than wonderful?"[16] Thoreau, like the carvers, had a special communion with wood. For Thoreau, it was a simple woodpile springing from his hand and axe that provided him a "value more permanent and universal than that of gold." For the carvers, it is a simple wooden chain connecting man to nature and culture, to social value and homespun beauty.

Epilogue

I ENDED my interviews where I began them—with George Blume. He moved more slowly now, and his hearing and eyesight had deteriorated. But his smile was quick as ever. It was too cold to talk on the porch, so we went into the living room. But inside, out of the open air he loved, George sat like an uninvited guest. "Well, you see, usually I'm outside or I just go in my room and that's it," he tried to explain. The house hardly told of his presence. A wooden fence he made lined the bottom of the Christmas tree, and a coat rack he had made stood in his bedroom, but his daughter had stored away a chain he had carved years ago. "Did you see my stuff over there?" he asked me, pointing with a frail hand toward Adyeville.

Too weak to make the trip to see the carvings' new home, he could still imagine them as they used to be in his basement. He asked about them as parents inquire about their children, with pride, concern, and hope.

"Yes sir, that was darn stuff, wasn't it? I had this one chain, did you see it, as small as a bitty watch chain and another as big as a, uh. . . . " He paused. He pushed his heavy glasses back. "I'm glad you're telling people about that, you know. Yep, I get homesick for that stuff."

I felt a tinge of sadness, so the laugh that followed surprised me. A red glow rose in his face as he crowed, "That was some kind of bullshit, huh?" True, you couldn't use his chains to hoist or haul, but they were hardly frivolous. He was telling me in his own way how important they were for him. When I said goodbye, he replied with a grin, "Well, I *hope* to be here."

I drove away through a crowd of factories heading for the rolling countryside beyond. I now saw this landscape of contrasts with newly-opened eyes, thanks to George and the others. In my rear-view mirror, I read a sign, "Welcome to Jasper, Nation's Wood Capital"—a reference to the city's many furniture companies. In the shadow of their commercial facades, informal woodcarving goes on in homes and yards. The carving lacks billboards, but it is itself a sign of the experience of workers, the knowledge they have acquired and hope to pass on, and their struggle to retain control over what they make.

George hangs on. He wrote me letters reporting the exact number of snowfalls and the average temperatures in Huntingburg. He bemoaned the state of the country. Then he turned to his own state. "Well, anyway I see you are living yet so I am only giting a little older. Lots of people ask me "How are you?" Well, I tell them the old Gray mare ain't what she used to be." Nine months later the same subjects were on his mind. "Well Simon we are having lots of hot weather. Around 100 degrees every day since middle of July. If it git as cold as we had heat we will have a hell of a winter. Well I am giting a little old, 85 this coming January. Excuse me for the mistakes I may be writing. I can't see out of my left eye on account of the cataracts." In early 1984, he wrote to say that his legs "want to give out," but he received a walker and kept going, if ever more slowly. His daughter takes him to the post office, but he wrote, "I don't see many people who were around." He closed, "Still use the front porch a lot."

George dealt with his maladies matter of factly. He knew that aging would bring that, after all. But aging also brought other priorities. He still had work ahead of him. He still had stories to tell, gardens to mow, widows to visit, and the world to think about. He used the immunity of old age to boldly speak his mind. He enjoyed the growth and independence of his age. He was a professional at aging. It was a career to him, much as working at the factory was a job that entailed standards and customs to follow. He would not be put on display at a festival or exhibit. His duties lay on the route from his home to the post office and back. He did not retire as much as change careers.

Floyd Bennington is finding new life in his later years. He has become a man to visit, a craftsman and teacher emeritus. The local paper carried a feature article on his carving, and community groups such as his Kiwanis Club ask him to talk about one-room schools, carving, and the way things used to be. Former students, now grown and well into their careers, come around to catch up occasionally.

Other time is devoted to his family. Floyd finds less time than he used to for carving, but he did complete one special carving for a friend who helped relieve his back pain. Floyd is training a young apprentice carver, so he knows his knowledge will endure, even after he is gone.

Earnest Bennett is even more active now than when I interviewed him. Another professional, like George Blume, at his craft and his age, he carves and travels with zeal. Earnest uses his time to see new sights and reach out to outlying family. He develops and demonstrates his carving skill, and takes part in organizing other carvers. A letter from him gives some idea of this indefatigable man. "We have had a busy year. Back from a six week trip at Sanibel Island, Florida, in February. Also visited with some of our relations in Louisville, Nashville, Tennessee, and a nephew . . . at Tifton, Georgia. We continue our work at the Children's Museum, doing several shows around the country and taught wood carving to twenty-one fourth-grade boys at vacation bible school for two weeks. Finished five projects. Very thankful—not one cut hand or finger in the whole time." In late 1983 he was busy making an elaborate chain requested for a United States Information Agency exhibit of folk art travelling to American embassies in Eastern Europe.

Wandley Burch died on June 25, 1983. Before he died, he had received the recognition he had looked for from the academic community. My visits and articles brought him attention he deserved and wanted. Students came around to see his work. The Folk Arts Program of the Indiana Arts Commission filled their brochure with photographs of him at work. A report published by the National Council for the Traditional Arts had a photograph of his carved "pinchers." A local cable station did a segment on him for their folk artists series. Wandley was a man who used chains to connect his friends and family to him, and to show pride in the traditions he grew up with. He teased others with the knowledge he had, but for me he unveiled his secrets. He died, having given life and meaning to his objects.

No death bells need toll for chain carving. "My uncle does that" people tell me regularly, and they ask, with some bewilderment, "What is it about that stuff?" The popular movie *Best Little Whorehouse in Texas* showed Burt Reynolds, as Sheriff Ed Earls, carving a chain; the carving symbolized a state of harmony in his town. *Time*, reporting on life in North Carolina, told of a man who "whittles

Burt Reynolds, as sheriff in *The Best Little Whorehouse in Texas*, carves a chain

Glen Van Antwerp with his peacock

chains, swords, canes and slingshots, and claims in the doing that it puts his mind to rest."[1] Such carving receives more public attention today through folk art exhibits and festivals. Michigan State University's museum put on a show of carved fans, including many made by three generations of Van Antwerps. The Central Oregon Folklife Festival featured the woodwork of Ray Pamperian who held odd jobs and hoboed. "Ray learned to carve items like the small pliers and various puzzles with movable parts from a single block of wood."[2] I also hear of chain carving with a modern twist—cutting a chain out of a tree log with a chainsaw. One report came from upstate New York where a log chain was made outside a bar on a bet, and another came from a student who told me of one done on his remote military base in Alaska. "Passed the time," the student said, "and besides, doing things like that kept you from going crazy."

Faded clippings of newspaper stories on chain carvers are sent to me, and in the light of what I found out from the men I interviewed, the stories now make more sense. A brief column on elderly Dave Strausser, a Shoemakersville, Pennsylvania, chain carver appeared in the Philadelphia evening newspaper, July 17, 1940, for example. The anonymous writer told of a four-foot chain Strausser made out of cedar. It took Strausser fifty-three weeks, working an average of two hours a day. Caged balls, pliers, and swivels were also in his repertoire, but he specialized in the chain. "A sickness, a malady?" the writer asked. No, it was a relief, a reaction against the routine of his factory job, the inspection of knitting and sewing machinery. "Sometimes he gets so mad at a sewing or a knitting machine that refuses to be fixed he feels like tossing it out the window, he says. Then it is a great relief, smiles he, to get back to wood carving. Even today, when he has access to modern tools, Mr. Strausser prefers the equipment he used as a boy." Strausser's techniques and motives sound familiar. "His elaborate combinations of chains and links and wheels-in-wheels are cut from a single piece of wood. He never uses a pattern." He may not use one, but he is part of one. His things come not out of clockwork, but handwork. "Whittling rests the nerves, he says. And he likes to point out that the things he makes are of no earthly use. Once when he was working on a matchstick chain, he found that one of the last links had a flaw in it and would not hold together. He didn't crack, he says, but he couldn't get it out of his mind for weeks and weeks. 'It takes just two things,' said Mr. Strausser, 'time and patience. People want to do things such a hurry now-a-days, they seem to have forgotten what every old wood-carver knows.' "

From what the old woodcarver knows, we can learn personal lessons. From knowing the woodcarver, we find social issues to ponder. For one, despite a popular image of technological hegemony in the United States, people still insist on maintaining the roles of folk crafts. We preserve creativity that is informally learned and executed, and we long for the vicarious control and compassion that the handmade folk object gives. We value tradition for the connection it gives us to people, places, and the past. Even if we don't practice the craft ourselves, we rely on its symbols. Wandley Burch's anvil no longer rang with hammer and tong, but it sparked his memory and identity.

Dave Strausser, Pennsylvania, and his carvings, ca. 1940

We can learn much from the satisfactions people find in folk process and design. Assembly lines boast efficiency but often at the expense of worker pride and identity. Time, rather than task, measures work in industry. The worker worries about completing the day rather than improving the quality of the product. "Chain carving is hard work, all right, but it's work you want to do," Earnest Bennett remarked. Although it is "work," Earnest wants to do it because he exercises control over the product and its design. The chain carver's work setting reflects his personality and he feels a personal stake in perfecting the product he creates. He is absorbed in himself, yet he shares his tradition with others. His workmanship in creating his object gives a sense of wholeness to his life and surroundings. He is a craftsman and he takes pride in the role. Some businesses now apply the characteristics of folk craft and art to improve the workplace. To humanize the job, they allow workers to control steps of production and design. Workspaces are opened up rather than partitioned, which enhances social interaction, contributes to a feeling of playfulness at work, and allows expressions of personal identity and aesthetics.[3]

Another lesson can be gained from relating creativity to different ages. Children, for example, learn manual skills and develop aesthetics in creating tree houses, folded paper sculptures, rock designs, and other artistic endeavors common to childhood. Their creations are temporary and do not receive much adult, or ethnographic, notice. They do not enter museum collections. Yet the making of them—as a statement of control and connection—influences the social psychological development of the child.

Folk objects are especially telling of social and psychological development, since they come out of shared experiences and they bespeak hidden feelings. The informality of these objects point to the poignancy of personal values and ideals. What people say through objects can break through the silence of growth and living. In an exhibit of older artists at New York's Pratt Institute, the curators commented, "At the end of the human life cycle, there is time for creative work as the pressure of earning a living is removed. Creativity, heretofore considered frivolous, is now a means to structure and fill the final years."[4] Another exhibit of aged artists had another interpretation of creativity's appeal to the elderly. It was a way to displace tragedy of death and pain common in their lives. That is only part of the story, I found, but what is significant is the reflection that often accompanies creativity. Some artists go through a life-review process as they work, "allowing the reintegration of difficult events from the past with present experiences. For all, creativity is a link between past and present and gives a sense of continuity and community."[5] Creativity is the common thread through all ages, but worthy of our attention is the motivation that draws old people to material arts. We can increasingly see the use of creativity as adaptation. The craftsmen are adapting to changing ways of doing things and viewing things. They are adapting themselves to a new stage of life. As people age, the objects they create change and their reasons for creating change, but the underlying aesthetics they developed in childhood and share with others in adulthood influence how they view the world and how they alter it.[6]

To the carvers, making wooden chains was appropriate to their

age and place, and their sex. It was something men have traditionally done. Handling the knife and cutting the rough wood was a man's
thing to do. Indeed, categories of masculinity and femininity come
to the surface in folk crafts. While the wives of the carvers preferred
working with the softer textures and colorful forms of cloth and food,
the men chose the firmer, rougher textures and natural tones of wood
and metal. The things made by the women brought them inside the
house; the men's things brought them outside. Chains stood out on
a carver's bench, for they signalled ways men have done things. Retired, at home with his wife, or all alone, the carver looked to creativity to reaffirm his masculinity.

We are becoming more aware of how the cultural context of being a man or woman influences the built world. If thinking about
creativity in terms of certain ages considers the *span* of creativity,
then the different arts of men and women involve the *spheres* of
creativity. These spheres intersect, but separate areas are maintained.
Anthropologist Marie Jeanne Adams noticed that in African societies
men carve images in wood, whereas women do not. She thought that
men's preference for wood and the restriction against carving wood
for women were universal. She considered carving figures and the
uses to which they were put by men to be parallel to giving birth by
women.[7] The figures, and chains, are given birth in a sense; they are
brought out from the wood, caressed, and raised. This assumes that
men imitate the women's sphere, rather than develop their own. What
is universal is the desire to externalize and dramatize one's persona
onto both living beings and inanimate objects. Both women and men
want to bring creations alive, and our choice of media in old age often
follows patterns established in childhood. Men learn early that wood,
the outdoors, handtools, and carving are manly. The categories stay
in mind and help shape the man's sphere of creativity. His workshop
gives him a place to call his own, a place to shape an identity.

I saw carving as an expression of sincere men, and I came to
realize something about public attitudes toward their work. Too often
people take apparently playful items and activities lightly, not realiz-
ing that they are framed by play precisely because they touch on sensitive issues and express deep-seated values. Art and play have much
in common, both allowing room for expression and fantasy, while
commenting on reality. Being expressive and not strictly utilitarian,
art and play convey symbolism, and the farther from conscious

awareness, the more that symbolism has to tell and the more it needs interpretation.

In most studies of crafts, interpretation is attempted through a type of history. Find the origin. Trace the development. Show the decline. Although such chronology establishes precedent and helps us organize our material, it rarely provides explanation and it avoids cultural criticism. For both we have to know the actors of cultural dramas; we have to know their motives and the immediate conditions that influence them; we have to recognize the psychological significance of creativity in different social situations shaped by the minutiae of experience. Creativity heightens senses and perceptions of shape and arrangement—and social structures. It brings hand, tool, wood, eye, and thought into a system that connects idea to design and meaning to production. Interpretation involves seeing the world from the creator's eyes, and stepping back from the creator for a wider perspective. Interpretation demands grasping how our bodies and minds work as part of culture, and how our objects project ourselves and in turn influence us.

Effective interpretation should lead to some personal reflection and social application. I, for one, could begin with my father. He was a "working man." He didn't know anything else. He cursed the cabs he drove for a living, but kept at it for the money and independence it brought. Forced into an early retirement by heart trouble, he was miserable. He would be home, not knowing what to do with himself. "I've got to work," he would tell me, but he knew it could kill him. He needed to find a creative outlet, but he had never developed one over the years. He is trying now, but with great difficulty because his ravaged childhood in concentration camps during World War II did not foster creative models for him to turn back to in later life. For Alois Schuch of Jasper, Indiana, creativity filled his last days. I heard from his daughter just before his death from cancer in November 1983. He had pain, but his carvings soothed him. She wrote, "He remembered when you used to visit and look at all the things he made. He has some wood chains and wants you to see them." I received his links, and they loomed large before me. They gave him purpose. When the words can no longer be spoken and the hands can no longer touch, his objects preserve his spirit.

Those whose goals are to help people adjust to abrupt social and physical change can benefit from understanding the uses and limits

Chains made by Alois Schuch, 1983

of creativity.[8] Indeed, the principles of folk art have direct application in art therapy and education. Creative objects often state a problem, technical and emotional, and suggest a remedy. Given to personal choice and emotional involvement, the things individuals create
which call on tradition can become symbolic autobiographies for use
in evaluating decision-making, reliant as they are on a sense of self
and connection with others. Objects do not have to be made to be
analytically read. In use and display, objects carry symbols and af-
fect the way viewers think and feel. Such symbols can be powerful.
Recall how George Blume's chains could evoke strong emotions for
Bert King. People rely on symbols imparted through creativity to express their deepest emotions, their gravest concerns, and their most
poignant, unutterable thoughts.

Creativity is another voice speaking your mind. When you cannot confront the conflicts within you or between you and the world, you can still comment on them, and maybe resolve them in using your hands to make unusual things. Creativity allows you to act out roles and images on a stage once removed from sullen reality. The object thus brought into being gives clues to the forces that drove its creation.

Beginning as form, the wooden chain becomes symbol when it conveys something important and personal. The object, in turn, can make one's life symbolic of values and ideals. What such heightened symbols stand for in human nature can be likened to a lion roaming wild and free. The object cages the symbols so as to contain the lion's wrath and to let the viewer imagine the surroundings and conditions from which they came. Chained, the lion seems less threatening, even playful, but the lion, or the symbol, roars more loudly, *if* we listen.

"Part of you is in a carving see; there's something there that goes with it," Floyd said. His carving, his creativity, brought his persona alive and it also conveyed a way of life, a way of thinking, wrought by his hands. The things he made will always have valuable lessons to give as long as we can connect lives to objects and minds to culture. The hope of describing creativity in human terms is that we may yet know the meaning of things for the individual and society. To know that meaning is to grasp ideas from which links are made.

Notes

PROLOGUE

1. Scandinavian chains are found in Iona Plath, *The Decorative Arts of Sweden* (New York: Charles Scribner's Sons, 1948), 157; E.J. Tangerman, *1001 Designs for Whittling and Woodcarving* (New York: McGraw-Hill, 1976), 40; Janice S. Stewart, *The Folk Arts of Norway* (New York: Dover, 1972), 85; Charles Holme, *Peasant Art in Sweden, Lapland and Iceland* (London: The Studio, 1910), plates 14,138. For Wales, England, and other European examples, see Edward H. Pinto, *Treen and Other Bygones* (London: G. Bell and Sons, 1969), 158-64, 299-325.

2. See Walter W. Battiss et al, *The Art of Africa* (Pietermaritzburg: Shuter and Shuter, 1958), 82-127; William H. Wiggins, "The Wooden Chains That Bind: A Look at One Shared Creation of Two Diaspora Woodcarvers," In *Black People and Their Culture: Selected Writing from the African Diaspora*, ed. Linn Shapiro (Washington, D.C.: Smithsonian Institution, 1976), 29-32; John Michael Vlach, *The Afro-American Tradition in Decorative Arts* (Cleveland: Cleveland Museum of Art, 1978), 31-32.

3. Assad Nadim, "Testing Cybernetics in Khan-El-Khalili: A Study of Arabesque Carpenters" (Ph.D. diss., Indiana University, 1975), 122; A. Viires, *Woodworking in Estonia* (Jerusalem: Israel Program for Scientific Translations, 1969), 80; P. Galaune, *Medžio Dirbiniai I Knyga Lietuvių Liaudies Menas* (Vilnius: Valstybine Grozines Literaturos Leidykla, 1956), plates 196, 342, 373, 374; Alexander K. Tschekalow, *Bauerliche russiche Holzkultur* (Dresden VEB Verlag der Kunst, 1967), plate 22; E. J. Tangerman, *Whittling and Woodcarving* (1936; reprint ed., New York, Dover, 1962), 91; Will Bondhus, "Carving a Ball Inside a Ball," *National Carvers Review* 9 (1978): 33-35 (China). Also from China is a pendant with chains made out of a solid piece of white nephrite at the Indianapolis Museum of Art (71.11.112). See also Marian Klamkin and Charles Klamkin, *Wood Carvings: North American Folk Sculptures* (New York: Hawthorn, 1974), 179.

4. Erwin O. Christensen, *Early American Wood Carving* (Cleveland: The World Publishing Co., 1952), 106; Priscilla Sawyer Lord and Daniel J. Foley, *The Folk Arts and Crafts of New England* (Philadelphia: Chilton, 1965), 26; correspondence from Frank G. White, curator, Old Sturbridge Village, 20 May 1980.

5. Philip V.R. Tilney, *Artifacts from the CCFCS Collections* (Ottawa: National Museum of Man Mercury Series, Canadian Centre for Folk Culture Studies Paper No. 5, 1973), 35-36; Nancy-Lou Gellermann Patterson, *Swiss-German and Dutch-German*

Mennonite Traditional Art in the Waterloo Region, Ontario (Ottawa: National Museum of Man Mercury Series, Canadian Centre for Folk Culture Studies Paper No. 27, 1979), 104-05. The Indiana University Museum has two chains carved out of solid blocks of ivory by Eskimos from St. Lawrence Island (17-27-CHI, 17-12-HSI). For Afro-American chains, see Vlach, 31-32; Wiggins, 29-32. The 1790 black-made chain was described in correspondence from James Nottage, assistant museum director, Kansas State Historical Society, 25 July 1980.

6. See Henry Glassie, *Pattern in the Material Folk Culture of the Eastern United States* (Philadelphia: University of Pennsylvania Press, 1968), 64-124; Milton Newton, "Cultural Preadaptation and the Upland South," *Geoscience and Man* 5 (1974): 143-54.

7. Based on information in correspondence from Stephen Williams, director, Wayne County, Indiana Historical Society Museum, 8 November 1978; correspondence from Michael P. O'Lear, curator, Indianapolis Children's Museum, 1 June 1980. Chain carvings along the route of southern migration can be found in Kenneth Clarke and Ira Kohn, *Kentucky's Age of Wood* (Lexington: University Press of Kentucky, 1976), 65-67; Patrick Huehls, "Lloyd Huehls: Whittling" (typescript, Indiana University Folklore Archives, 1972); Vicki Chulock, "Folk Wood Carving and Related Wood Craft" (typescript, Indiana University Folklore Archives, 1968); Klamkin and Klamkin, 185.

8. See Elfrieda Lang, "German Immigration to Dubois County, Indiana, during the Nineteenth Century," *Indiana Magazine of History* 41 (1945): 131-51; Charles Van Ravenswaay, *The Arts and Architecture of German Settlers in Missouri: A Vanishing Culture* (Columbia: University of Missouri Press, 1977), 401-06; Katherine C. Grier, *Celebrations in Wood: The Sculpture of John Scholl (1927-1916)* (Harrisburg, Pennsylvania: William Penn Memorial Museum, 1979).

9. Steven Banks, *The Handicrafts of the Sailor* (New York: Arco, 1974).

10. Correspondence from R.C. Malley, assistant registrar, Mystic Seaport Museum, 30 May 1980.

11. Marsha MacDowell and C. Kurt Dewhurst, "Expanding Frontiers: The Michigan Folk Art Project," *Perspectives on American Folk Art*, ed. Ian M. G. Quimby and Scott Swank (New York: W.W. Norton, 1980). 54-78; Suzi Jones, *Oregon Folklore* (Eugene: Oregon Arts Commission, 1977).

12. Jesse Corbin, a Bedford, Indiana, stone-chain carver is reported in "Skill and Perseverance," *Quarries and Mills* 1 (1930): 6. Two giant links carved out of limestone stand on a statue on the grounds of the Monroe County Courthouse, Bloomington, Indiana. Dan Ward at Bowling Green State University wrote me (14 August 1980) with a description of a chain carved out of a ten-foot log in Long Lake, New York. Another chainsaw sculptor, Richard Leeth, is covered in *Ohio Folk Traditions: A New Generation* by Alan Govenar (Lancaster, Ohio: Fairfield County District Library, 1981). Tina Bucuvalas, a graduate student at the University of California at Los Angeles, told me that Peter Voorheis, a fellow student, gave her a paper-clip chain as a friendship token when he left UCLA in 1977. Jan Brunvand describes gum-wrapper chains in *A Guide for Collectors of Folklore in Utah* (Salt Lake City: University of Utah Press, 1971), 102-03. See also Mary and Herbert Knapp, *One Potato, Two Potato . . . : The Secret Education of American Children* (New York: W.W.Norton, 1976). 259.

CHAPTER ONE

1. Folklorists compare prominent motifs in collected narratives to spotlight recurrent traditional ideas of content and composition. Cf. motifs D1389.2 Charms against theft, D1817.0.1.1 Witch (wizard) reveals name of thief, D1817.0.1.3 Wizard compels thief to return stolen property, from Stith Thompson, *Motif-Index of Folk Literature* (revised ed.; Bloomington: Indiana Univ. Press, 1975). See also Edward von Hoffmann-Krayer and Hanns Bächtold-Staübli, *Handwörterbuch des deutschen Aberglaubens* (*HDA*), 10 vols. (Berlin: Walter de Gruyter, 1927-42), I:875, s.v. "Bannen."

2. Cf. motifs G265.4.1.1 Witch causes death of cattle, G224.3 Witches get their powers from books, from Earnest W. Baughman, *Type and Motif-Index of the Folktales of England and North America* (The Hague: Mouton, Indiana University Folklore Series No. 20, 1966); *HDA* I, 1692, s.v. "Buche." Cf. also no. 7625 Cows and calves may be killed by the casting of a spell, from Wayland Hand, ed., *The Frank C. Brown Collection of North Carolina Folklore, Popular Beliefs and Superstitions from North Carolina* (Durham, North Carolina: Duke University Press, 1961) and "charm breaking 7D, by threatening the witch," from Christine Goldberg, "Traditional American Witch Legends: A Catalog," *Indiana Folklore* 7 (1974): 77-108.

3. Cf. Thompson motif G272.7.2 Broom across door protects from witch; Brown no. 5595 Anyone who refuses to step over a broom is a witch, no. 5596 Lay a broom down in the doorway when you see company coming, no. 5634 If you want to keep witches away, lay a straw broom in the doorway. Cf. also no. 9525 Woman cannot step over broom—German, from Harry Middleton Hyatt, *Folk-Lore from Adams County, Illinois* (New York: Memoirs of the Alma Egan Hyatt Foundation 1935); Wayland D. Hand, "Popular Beliefs and Superstitions from Pennsylvania," *Keystone Folklore Quarterly* 4 (1959): 106-20, no. 186; *HDA* I 1135, 1138-39, III 1899, 1903, 1909; Edwin Miller Fogel, *Beliefs and Superstitions of the Pennsylvania Germans* (Philadelphia: Americana Germanica, 1915), no. 640.

4. Cf. Baughman motifs G265.6.3(a) Witches causes horse to balk, D2072.0.2.1 Horse enchanted so that he stands still; Thompson motif D2063.1.1 Tormenting by sympathetic magic. Person (usually witch) tormented by abusing an animal or object; D 1654.12 Horse magically becomes immovable; Hyatt no. 9305 Team of horses balk, no. 9306 Horses balk, driver takes neck yoke and hits hack real hard, witch drops dead—Terman; *HDA* I 878. Cf. also "The Magic Calk" in *Folktales of Hungary*, ed. Linda Dégh (Chicago: Univ. of Chicago Press, 1965), 243-47.

5. The structuring power of belief and narrative on a society is discussed further in Janet Langlois, "Belle Gunness, The Lady Bluebeard: Community Legend as Metaphor," *Journal of the Folklore Institute* 15 (1978): 147-60.

6. For further discussion of the structure of belief performance, see Michael Edward Bell, "Pattern, Structure, and Logic in Afro-American Hoodoo Performance" (Ph.D. diss., Indiana University, 1980); Linda Dégh and Andrew Vázsonyi, "Legend and Belief," in *Folklore Genres*, ed. Dan Ben-Amos (Austin: Univ. Of Texas Press, 1976), 93-124.

7. See Rebecca Conrad, "The Family Farm: A Study of Folklife in Historical Context," *MidAmerica Folklore* 7 (1979): 69-76; Joe R. Motheral, "The Family Farm and the Three Traditions," *Journal of Farm Economics* 33 (1951): 514-20; Paul H. Landis, *Rural Life in Process* (New York: McGraw-Hill, 1940).

8. Richard M. Dorson, "Heart Disease and Folklore," in *Readings in American Folklore*, ed. Jan Harold Brunvand (New York: W.W. Norton, 1979), 137.

9. For examples of how modernity reinforces older folk beliefs, see Ellen J. Stekert, "Focus for Conflict: Southern Mountain Medical Beliefs in Detroit," in *The Urban Experience and Folk Tradition*, ed. Américo Pardes and Ellen J. Stekert (Austin: University of Texas Press, 1971). 95-127; Gary Fine, "The Kentucky Fried Rat: Legends and Modern Society," *Journal of the Folklore Institute* 17 (1980): 222-43; Robertson Davies, "A Few Kind Words for Superstition," *Newsweek* (20 November 1978): 23; Ronald L. Baker, "The Influence of Mass Culture on Modern Legends," *Southern Folklore Quarterly* 40 (1976): 367-76.

10. A discussion of the significance of such adjustments is found in J.A.C. Brown, *The Social Psychology of Industry* (1954; reprint ed., New York: Penguin Books, 1980), especially pp. 269-75; Morton Leeds, "The Process of Cultural Stripping and Reintegration: The Rural Migrant in the City," in *The Urban Experience and Folk Tradition*, ed. Paredes and Stekert, 165-76; Landis, *Rural Life*.

11. Henry Glassie, *Passing the Time in Ballymenone* (Philadelphia: Univ. Of Pennsylvania Press, 1982), 423-24.

12. Thomas Hart Benton, *An Artist in America*, 4th rev. ed. (Columbia: Univ. Of Missouri Press, 1983), 25-26.

13. Richard M. Dorson, "Comments on the History of Folkloristics" *Midwestern Journal of Language and Folklore* 3 (1977): 53.

14. Michael Owen Jones, *The Hand Made Object and Its Maker* (Berkeley: Univ. of California Press, 1975), 165-66.

15. Sigmund Freud, *Civilization and Its Discontents* (New York: W.W. Norton, 1961), 26-27.

16. Harriette Arnow, *The Dollmaker* (1954; reprint, New York: Avon, 1972), 377.

17. Aldous Huxley, *Point Counter Point*, Modern Library ed. (New York: Doubleday Doran, 1928), 54.

18. *Celebration: A World of Art and Ritual* (Washington, D.C.: Smithsonian Institution Press, 1982) 15.

19. Kenneth L. Ames, *Beyond Necessity: Art in the Folk Tradition* (New York: W.W. Norton, 1977), 27-30. See also Richard Hofstadter, "The Myth of the Happy Yoeman," in *American Vistas*, ed. Leonard Dinnerstein and Kenneth Jackson (New York: Oxford Univ. Press, 1971), 20-32.

CHAPTER TWO

1. Samuel G. Goodrich, *Recollections of a Lifetime*, 2 vols. (New York: Miller, Orton and Mulligan, 1856), I: 92-93.

2. See Robert Pawlowski, " 'Where's Your Knife?': The Disappearance of the Pocketknife," *Mississippi Folklore Register* 13 (1979): 5-9.

3. Examples are "A Whittler Champ," *Popular Science Monthly* (May 1927): 64; John Draper, "$1,000 in Cash Offered to Whittlers," *Popular Mechanics* (January 1932): 7-8; William Harvest, "How to Whittle Interlocked Rings," *Popular Science Monthly* (December 1932), 70.

4. These terms are discussed further in James B. Johnstone, *Woodcarving Techniques and Projects* (Menlo Park, California: Lane, 1971), 16.

5. Cecil W. Houlton, *Whittling Wooden Variety Chains* (Monte Vista, Colorado: C.B.I. Offset, 1972), 6.

6. Terms for grips and cuts from Johnstone, *Woodcarving Techniques*, 14-15.

7. For more discussion, see Joseph H. Krause, *The Nature of Art* (Englewood Cliffs, New Jersey: Prentice-Hall, 1969), 261-95; Henry Glassie, "Folk Art," in *Folklore and Folklife: An Introduction*, ed. Richard M. Dorson (Chicago: University of Chicago Press, 1972), 253-80; Simon J. Bronner, "The Anglo-American Aesthetic," in *Encyclopedia of Southern Culture*, ed. William Ferris and Charles Wilson (Chapel Hill: University of North Carolina Press, forthcoming).

8. Harriette Arnow, *The Dollmaker*, 490.

9. This view is based on the philosophy of George Herbert Mead. See especially his "The Nature of Aesthetic Experience," *The International Journal of Ethics* 36 (1926): 382-93; *The Philosophy of the Present*, ed. Arthur E. Murphy (Chicago: Univ. of Chicago Press, 1932); *On Social Psychology*, ed. Anselm Stauss (Chicago: Univ. of Chicago Press, 1964). I comment further on some of his ideas in "Toward a Philosophy of Folk Objects: A Praxic Perspective," in *Personal Places: Perspectives on Informal Art Environments*, ed. Daniel Franklin Ward (Bowling Green, Ohio: Bowling Green Univ. Popular Press, 1984). See also a modern study of the relation of transactions between symbols and self by Mihaly Csikszentmihalyi and Eugene Rochberg-Halton in *The Meaning of Things* (Cambridge: Cambridge Univ. Press, 1981).

10. Henry Glassie, *Folk Housing in Middle Virginia* (Knoxville: Univ. of Tennessee Press, 1975), 134.

11. This is partly why Michael Owen Jones argues that despite the growing march of factory production, a demand for handmade goods will always exist. See his excellent study, *The Hand Made Object and Its Maker* (Berkeley: Univ. of California Press, 1975), 200. See also my "The Haptic Experience of Culture," *Anthropos* 77 (1982): 351-62, and for a general overview, see Charles Camp, ed., *Traditional Craftsmanship in America* (Washington, D.C.: National Council for the Traditional Arts, 1983).

12. See Roger Abrahams, "The Literary Study of the Riddle," *Texas Studies in Literature and Language* 14 (1972): 188-89.

13. Roger Abrahams and Alan Dundes, "Riddles," in *Folklore and Folklife*, ed. Dorson, 137-38.

14. Ian Hamnett, "Ambiguity, Classification and Change: The Function of Riddles," *Man* 2 (1967): 387.

15. Robert Plant Armstrong, *The Powers of Presence* (Philadelphia: University of Pennsylvania Press, 1981), 5.

16. See Calvin Trillin, "Simon Rodia: Watts Towers" *Naives and Visionaries* (New York: E. P. Dutton, 1974), 21-31.

17. Jones, *The Hand Made Object*, 1-25; idem, "A Strange Rocking Chair . . . The Need to Express, The Urge to Create," *Folklore and Mythology* 2 (November 1982): 1, 4-7.

18. Barbara Wahl Kaufman, *A Sampling of Folk Art* (South Orange, N.J.: Seton Hall University, 1983).

19. Allen Eaton and Lucinda Crile, *Rural Handicrafts in the United States* (Washington, D.C.: U.S. Department of Agriculture, 1946).

20. E. J. Tangerman, *Whittling and Woodcarving* (1907; reprint, New York: Dover, 1962), 74.

CHAPTER THREE

1. I interviewed Alois Schuch in 1978 and 1979. For more discussion of his carving, see Alice Morrison Mordoh, "Two Woodcarvers: Jasper, Dubois County, Indiana," *Indiana Folklore* 12 (1980): 17-29.

2. For examples, see Alan Dundes and Carl Pagter, *Work Hard and You Shall Be Rewarded* (Bloomington: Indiana University Press, 1978).

3. Allen H. Eaton, *Handicrafts of the Southern Highlands* (1937 rpt., New York: Dover, 1973), 180.

4. Robert Sayers, "Traditional Southern Crafts in the Twentieth Century," in *Festival of American Folklife 1981*, ed. Jack Santino (Washington, D.C.: Smithsonian Institution, 1981), 17.

5. Anthony Storr, *The Dynamics of Creation* (New York: Atheneum, 1972), 44.

6. Carl R. Rogers, "Toward a Theory of Creativity," in *Creativity and its Cultivation*, ed. Harold H. Anderson (New York: Harper and Brothers, 1959), 79-80.

7. Storr, *The Dynamics of Creation*, 45.

8. Ibid., 48.

9. See John R. Nichols, "How Opiates Change Behavior," *Scientific American* 212 (February 1965): 81-88.

10. See Edward H. Pinto, *Treen or Small Woodenware Through the Ages* (London: B.T. Batsford, 1949), 62.

11. See Len Evans, *The Lore of the Love Spoon* (Cardiff, Wales: John Jones Cardiff Ltd., 1978), 8-9; *The Story of the Love Spoon* (Swansea, Wales: Celtic Educational Ltd., 1977), 89.

12. The carved spoons with chains are documented in Edward H. Pinto, *Treen and Other Bygones* (London: G. Bell and Sons, 1969), 158-64. "Spooning" in language is documented in Harold Wentworth and Stuart Berg Flexner, *Dictionary of American Slang* (New York: Thomas Y. Crowell, 1967), 510-11.

13. Barbara Myerhoff, *Number Our Days* (New York: Simon and Schuster, 1978), 251.

14. For other examples of "art for its own sake," see Michael Owen Jones, "L.A. Add-ons and Re-dos: Renovation in Folk Art and Architectural Design," in *Perspectives on American Folk Art*, ed. Ian M.G. Quimby and Scott T. Swank (New York: W.W. Norton, 1980), 325-63; Simon J. Bronner, "Manner Books and Suburban Houses: The Structure of Tradition and Aesthetics," *Winterthur Portfolio* 18 (1983): 61-68; Donald Van Horn, *Carved in Wood* (Batesville: Arkansas College Folklore Archive Publications, 1979); John Michael Vlach, *The Afro-American Tradition in the Decorative Arts* (Cleveland: Cleveland Museum of Art, 1978), 31-32; Marian Klamkin and Charles Klamkin, *Woodcarvings: North American Folk Sculptures* (New York: Hawthorn Books, 1974), 179-86.

15. Michael Owen Jones, *The Hand Made Object*, 242.

16. Henry David Thoreau, *Walden* (New York: Holt, Rinehart and Winston, 1964 ed.), 272-73.

EPILOGUE

1. Gregory Jones, "In North Carolina: Beware of Falling Cows," *Time* (18 April 1983), 12.

2. Dale Coats, "Seventy Years of Whittling," in *Central Oregon Folklife Festival,* ed. Suzi Jones (n.p., 1978), 27.

3. See Roy P. Fairchild, ed., *Humanizing the Workplace* (Buffalo, New York: Prometheus, 1974); Michael Owen Jones, "A Feeling for Form, as Illustrated by People at Work," in *Folklore on Two Continents,* ed. Nikolai Burlakoff and Carl Lindahl (Bloomington, Indiana: Trickster Press, 1980), 260-69; Bruce E. Nickerson, "Is There a Folk in the Factory?" *Journal of American Folklore* 87 (1974): 133-39; Michael J. Bell, "Tending Bar at Brown's: Occupational Role as Artistic Performance," *Western Folklore* 35 (1976): 93-107; Philip Nusbaum, "A Conversational Approach to Occupational Folklore: Conversation, Work, Play, and the Workplace," *Folklore Forum* 11 (1978): 18-28.

4. Amy Brook Snider, "The Education of the Elderly Artist," in *Images of Experience,* ed. Ellen Schwartz, Amy Snider, and Don Sunseri (New York: Pratt Institute, 1982),5.

5. Doris Francis-Erhard, *Older Cleveland Folk Artists* (Cleveland: The Department of Aging, n.d.), 4.

6. For discussions of aging and worldview, see Brian Sutton-Smith, "A Developmental Psychology of Play and the Arts," *Perspectives on Education* (Spring 1971): 8-17; Barre Toelken, *The Dynamics of Folklore* (Boston: Houghton Mifflin, 1979), 225-62; Margaret Clark and Barbara Gallatin Anderson, *Culture and Aging* (Springfield, Illinois: Charles C. Thomas, 1967); Alan Dundes, "Folk Ideas as Units of World View," in *Toward New Perspectives in Folklore,* ed. Américo Paredes and Richard Bauman (Austin: University of Texas Press 1972); Alan Jabbour, "Some Thoughts from a Folk Cultural Perspectives," in *Perspectives on Aging* (Cambridge, Mass.: Ballinger, 1982).

7. Marie Jeanne Adams, "Afterword. Spheres of Men's and Women's Creativity," *Ethnologische Zeitschrift Zurich* 1 (1980): 163-67.

8. For background on the argument given for applied folklore in this paragraph, see David Hufford, "Some Approaches to the Application of Folklore Studies," in *Papers on Applied Folklore,* ed. Dick Sweterlitsch (Folklore Forum Bibliographic and Special Studies, No. 8, 1971), 6-9; Cortland P. Auser, "The Viable Community: Redirections Through Applied Folklore," *New York Folklore Quarterly* 25 (1970): 3-13; Ellen J. Stekert, "Focus for Conflict: Southern Mountain Beliefs in Detroit," in *The Urban Experience and Folk Tradition,* ed. Américo Paredes and Ellen J. Stekert (Austin: University of Texas Press, 1971), 95-127; Toelken, *The Dynamics of Folklore,* 225-62; Michael Owen Jones, "Folk Art Production and the Folklorist's Obligation," *Journal of Popular Culture* 4 (1970): 194-212; Barbara Weber, "Folk Art as Therapy with a Group of Old People," *American Journal of Art Therapy* 20 (1981): 47-52.

Bibliography

This bibliography is intended to outline my influences, list my cited references, and suggest further readings on the subjects and ideas contained in the book. I have devised categories for the literature which were useful to me, and my hope is that they can be serviceable to fellow explorers.

GENERAL

Here are works that describe my region of study, provide background on material culture and folklore, and generally inspired my thinking.

Auser, Cortland P. "The Viable Community: Redirections Through Applied Folklore." *New York Folklore Quarterly* 25 (1970): 3-13.

Baker, Ronald L. "The Influence of Mass Culture on Modern Legends." *Southern Folklore Quarterly* 40 (1976): 367-76.

Barnhart, John D., and Donald F. Carmony. *Indiana: From Frontier to Industrial Commonwealth.* New York: Lewis Historical Publishing Company, 1954.

Baughman, Ernest W. *Type and Motif-Index of the Folktales of England and North America.* The Hague: Mouton, Indiana University Folklore Series No. 20, 1966.

Bauman, Richard, and Roger Abrahams, with Susan Kalčik. "American Folklore and American Studies." *American Quarterly* 28 (1976): 360-77.

Ben-Amos, Dan, ed. *Folklore Genres.* Austin: University of Texas Press, 1976.

Bernard, Jessie. "Observation and Generalization in Cultural Anthropology." *American Journal of Sociology* 50 (1945): 284-91.

Béteille, André, and T.N. Madan, eds. *Encounter and Experience: Personal Accounts of Fieldwork.* Honolulu: The University Press of Hawaii, 1975.

Boas, Franz. *Race, Language and Culture.* New York: The Free Press, 1940.

Boorstin, Daniel. *The Americans: The National Experience.* New York: Vintage Books, 1965.

Brewster, Paul, et al., eds. *Frank C. Brown Collection of North Carolina Folklore,* 7 vols. Durham: Duke University Press, 1952-64.

Bronner, Simon J. "Concepts in the Study of Material Aspects of American Folk Culture." *Folklore Forum* 12 (1979): 133-72.

_____. "Modern Anthropological Trends and Their Folkloristic Relationships." *Folk Life* 19 (1981): 66-83.

_____. " 'Visible Proofs': Material Culture Studies in American Folkloristics." *American Quarterly* 35 (1983): 315-38.

Bronner, Simon J., and Stephen P. Poyser, eds. *Approaches to the Study of Material Aspects of American Folk Culture*. Bloomington, Indiana: Folklore Forum Special Issue, 1979.

Browne, Ray B., and Ralph H. Wolfe, eds. *Directions and Dimensions in American Culture Studies in the 1980s*. Bowling Green, Ohio: Bowling Green University Popular Press, 1979.

Brunvand, Jan Harold. *A Guide for Collectors of Folklore in Utah*. Salt Lake City: University of Utah Press, 1971.

Carson, Cary. "Doing History with Material Culture." In *Material Culture and the Study of American Life*, ed. Ian M.G. Quimby, pp. 41-64. New York: W.W. Norton, 1978.

Chapple, Edward. "The Unbounded Reaches of Anthropology as a Research Science; and Some Working Hypotheses." *American Anthropologist* 82 (1980): 741-58.

Conrad, Rebecca. "The Family Farm: A Study of Folklife in Historical Context." *MidAmerica Folklore* 7 (1979): 69-76.

Dégh, Linda. *Folktales of Hungary*. Chicago: University of Chicago Press, 1965.

Dégh, Linda, and Andrew Vázsonyi. "Legend and Belief." In *Folklore Genres*, ed. Dan Ben-Amos, pp. 93-124. Austin: University of Texas Press, 1976.

Denby, Priscilla. "Self Discovered: The Car as Symbol in American Folklore and Literature." Ph.D. diss., Indiana University, 1981.

Dorson, Richard M. "A Southern Indiana Field Station." *Midwest Folklore* 11 (1961): 133-38.

_____. *Buying the Wind: Regional Folklore in the United States*. Chicago: University of Chicago Press, 1964.

_____. *American Folklore and the Historian*. Chicago: University of Chicago Press, 1971.

_____. *Folklore: Selected Essays*. Bloomington: Indiana University Press, 1972.

_____. "Concepts of Folklore and Folklife Studies." In *Folklore and Folklife: An Introduction*, ed. Richard M. Dorson, pp. 1-50. Chicago: University of Chicago Press, 1972.

_____. "Comments on the History of Folkloristics." *Midwestern Journal of Language and Folklore* 3 (1977): 50-53.

_____. "We All Need the Folk." *Journal of the Folklore Insititute* 15 (1978): 267-69.

Earle, Alice Morse. *Home Life in Colonial Days*. 1898; reprint ed., Stockbridge, Massachusetts: Berkshire Traveller Press, 1974.

Fairchild, Roy P. *Humanizing the Workplace*. Buffalo, New York: Prometheus, 1974.

Fine, Gary Alan. "The Kentucky Fried Rat: Legend and Modern Society." *Journal of the Folklore Institute* 17 (1980): 222-43.

Fogel, Edwin Miller. *Beliefs and Superstititons of the Pennsylvania Germans*. Philadelphia: Americana Germanica, 1915.

Glassie, Henry. *Pattern in the Material Folk Culture of the Eastern United States*. Philadelphia: University of Pennsylvania Press, 1968.

_____. "Meaningful Things and Appropriate Myths: The Artifact's Place in American Studies." In *Prospects 3: An Annual of American Culture Studies*, ed. Jack Salzman, pp. 1-49. New York: Burt Franklin, 1978.

————. *Passing the Time in Ballymenone: Culture and History of an Ulster Community.* Philadelphia: University of Pennsylvania Press, 1982.

Goldberg, Christine. "Traditional American Witch Legends: A Catalog." *Indiana Folklore* 7 (1974): 77-108.

Goodenough, Ward H. *Culture, Language, and Society.* Addison-Wesley Module in Anthropology, Number 7, 1971.

Hand. Wayland. "Popular Beliefs and Superstitions from Pennsylvania." *Keystone Folklore Quarterly* 4 (1959): 106-20.

Harris, Theodore L., and Wilson E. Schwahn. *Selected Readings on the Learning Process.* New York: Oxford University Press, 1961.

Hofstadter, Richard. "The Myth of the Happy Yeoman." In *American Vistas: 1877 to the Present,* ed. Leonard Dinnerstein and Kenneth T. Jackson, pp. 20-32. New York: Oxford University Press, 1971.

Hufford, David. "Some Approaches to the Application of Folklore Studies." In *Papers on Applied Folklore,* ed. Dick Sweterlitsch, pp. 6-9. Folklore Forum Bibliographic and Special Studies, No. 8, 1971.

Hyatt, Harry Middleton. *Folk-Lore From Adams County, Illinois.* New York: Alma Egan Hyatt Foundation, 1935.

Jones, Louis C. "Folk Culture and the Historical Society." *Minnesota History* 31 (1950): 11-17.

————. "Three Eyes on the Past: A New Triangulation for Local Studies." *New York Folklore Quarterly* 12 (1956): 3-13.

Kingsbury, Robert C. *An Atlas of Indiana.* Bloomington: Department of Geography, Indiana University, 1970.

Koenig, Otto. "Behaviour Study and Civilization." In *The Nature of Human Behaviour,* ed. Günter Altner, pp. 153-210. London: George Allen and Unwin, 1976.

Kouwenhoven, John A. "American Studies: Words or Things?" In *American Studies in Transition,* ed. Marshall W. Fishwick, pp. 15-35. Boston: Houghton Mifflin, 1964.

Kubler, George. *The Shape of Time: Remarks on the History of Things.* New Haven: Yale University Press, 1962.

Landis, Paul H. *Rural Life in Process.* New York: McGraw Hill, 1940.

Lang, Elfrieda. "German Immigration to Dubois County, Indiana During the Nineteenth Century." *Indiana Magazine of History* 41 (1945): 131-51.

————. "Conditions of Travel Experienced by German Immigrants to Dubois County, Indiana." *Indiana Magazine of History* 41 (1945): 327-44.

Langlois, Janet. "Belle Gunness, the Lady Bluebeard: Community Legend as Metaphor." *Journal of the Folklore Institute* 15 (1978): 147-60.

Leeds, Morton. "The Process of Cultural Stripping and Reintegration: The Rural Migrant in the City." In *The Urban Experience and Folk Tradition,* ed. Américo Paredes and Ellen J. Stekert, pp. 165-60. Austin: University of Texas Press, 1971.

Loomis, Ormond. "Tradition and the Individual Farmer: A Study of Folk Agricultural Practices in Southern Central Indiana." Ph.D. diss. Indiana University, 1980.

Lord, Albert B. *The Singer of Tales.* New York: Atheneum, 1978.

Merriam, Alan P. *The Anthropology of Music.* Evanston, Illinois: Northwestern University Press, 1964.

Montagu, Ashley. *Touching: The Human Significance of the Skin.* New York: Columbia University Press, 1971.

Motheral, Joe R. "The Family Farm and the Three Traditions." *Journal of Farm Economics* 33 (1951): 514-20.

Newton, Milton. "Cultural Preadaptation and the Upland South." *Geoscience and Man* 5 (1974): 143-54.

Nicolaisen, Wilhelm F.H. "The Folk and the Region." *New York Folklore* 2 (1976): 143-49.

————. " 'Distorted Function' in Material Aspects of Culture." *Folklore Forum* 12 (1979): 223-36.

Peate, Iorwerth C. "The Study of Folklife: and Its Part in the Defence of Civilization." *Gwerin* 2 (1959): 97-109.

Peckham, Howard H. "Impressions of Southern Indiana." *Indiana History Bulletin* 22 (1945): 181-83.

Rapoport, Amos. *House Form and Culture.* Englewood Cliffs, New Jersey: Prentice-Hall, 1969.

Riedl, Norbert. "Folklore vs. 'Volkskunde.'" *Tennessee Folklore Society Bulletin* 31 (1965): 47-53.

————. "Folklore and the Study of Material Aspects of Folk Culture." *Journal of American Folklore* 79 (1966): 557-63.

Roberts, Warren. "Field Work in Dubois County, Indiana: A Project of the Folklore Institute, Indiana University." *Echoes of History* 6 (1976): 12-14.

Santino, Jack, ed. *Festival of American Folklife 1981.* Washington, D.C.: Smithsonian Insititution, 1981.

Schlereth, Thomas J., ed. *Material Culture Studies in America.* Nashville: American Association for State and Local History, 1982.

Skramstad, Harold. "American Things: A Neglected Material Culture." *American Studies International* 10 (1972): 11-22.

Sonderman, Albert F. *Business Activities in Ferdinand, Dubois County, Southwestern Indiana.* Ferdinand: Albert F. Sondermann, 1965.

Sonderman, Louis, ed. *This, Our Town: Jasper, Indiana* Jasper: Jasper Centennial Corporation, 1966.

Spradley, James P., and Michael A. Rynkiewich, eds. *The Nacirema: Readings on American Culture.* Boston: Little, Brown and Company, 1975.

Stahl, Sandra K. "The Personal Narrative as Folklore." *Journal of the Folklore Institute* 14 (1977): 9-30.

Stekert, Ellen. "Focus for Conflict: Southern Medical Beliefs in Detroit." In *The Urban Experience and Folk Tradition,* ed. Américo Paredes and Ellen J. Stekert, pp. 95-127. Austin: University of Texas Press, 1971.

Stilgoe, John R. *Common Landscape of America, 1580-1845.* New Haven: Yale University Press, 1982.

Thompson, Stith. *Motif-Index of Folk-Literature.* Rev. ed., Bloomington: Indiana University Press, 1975.

Thoreau, Henry David. *Walden; or, Life in the Woods.* New York: Holt, Rinehart and Winston, 1964 ed.

Toelken, Barre. *The Dynamics of Folklore.* Boston: Houghton Mifflin, 1979.

Turner, Frederick Jackson. "Routes of Travel." In *Readings in Indiana History,* compiled by Gayle Thornbrough and Dorothy Riker, pp. 194-96. Indianapolis: Indiana Historical Bureau, 1967.

von Hoffman-Krayer, Edward, and Hanns Bächtold-Staübli. *Handwörterbuch des deutschen Aberglaubens*. 10 vols. Berlin: Walter de Gruyter, 1927-42.

Wentworth, Harold, and Stuart Berg Flexner. *Dictionary of American Slang*. New York: Thomas Y. Crowell, 1967.

Writers' Program, Indiana. *Indiana: A Guide to the Hoosier State*. New York: Oxford University Press, 1941.

Yoder, Don. "Folklife Studies in American Scholarship." In *American Folklife*, ed. Don Yoder, pp. 3-18. Austin: University of Texas Press, 1976.

Zwicky, Ann D., and Arnold M. Zwicky. "America's National Dish: The Style of Restaurant Menus." *American Speech* 55 (1980): 83-92.

THEORY AND METHOD

Drawing especially on behavioral and social sciences, I looked for interdisciplinary writings that revealed the workings of mind, expression, and behavior. I draw your attention particularly to the inspiring books of Michael Owen Jones, Henry Glassie, and George Herbert Mead. They, and the other publications on this list, do not share a single viewpoint, but together they contributed perspectives that helped shape my opinions.

Ames, Kenneth L. "Meaning in Artifacts: Hall Furnishings in Victorian America." *Journal of Interdisciplinary History* 9 (1978): 19-46.

Atkinson, J.W., ed. *Motivation and Fantasy Action in Society*. Princeton, New Jersey: van Nostrand, 1958.

Azadovski, Mark K. *Eine sibirsche Märchenzählerin*. Helsinki: Folklore Fellows Communication 68, 1926.

_____. "A Siberian Narrator." In *The Study of Russian Folklore*, ed. Felix Oinas and Stephen Soudakoff, pp. 79-89. The Hague: Mouton, 1975.

Bailis, Stanley. "The Social Sciences in American Studies: An Integrative Conception." *American Quarterly* 26 (1974): 202-24.

Bauman, Richard. "Toward a Behavioral Theory of Folklore." *Journal of American Folklore* 82 (1969): 167-70.

Bell, Michael J. "Tending Bar at Brown's: Occupational Role as Artistic Performance." *Western Folklore* 35 (1976): 93-107.

Ben-Amos, Dan. "Analytical Categories and Ethnic Genres." In *Folklore Genres*, ed. Dan Ben-Amos, pp. 215-42. Austin: University of Texas Press, 1976.

_____. "The Ceremony of Innocence." *Western Folklore* 38 (1979): 47-52.

Bidney, David. *Theoretical Anthropology*. New York: Columbia University Press, 1953.

Bringéus, Nils-Arvid. "The Communicative Aspect in Ethnology and Folklore." *Ethnologia Scandinavica* 9 (1979): 5-17.

Bronner, Simon J. "Reflections on Field Research in the Folklife Sciences." *New York Folklore* 6 (1980): 151-60.

_____. "The Paradox of Pride and Loathing, and Other Problems." *Western Folklore* 35 (1981): 115-24.

_____. "The Haptic Experience of Culture." *Anthropos* 77 (1982): 351-62.

_____. " 'Learning of the People': Folklorists in the Study of Behavior and Thought." *New York Folklore* 9 (1983): 75-88.

_____. "Toward a Philosophy of Folk Objects: A Praxic Perspective." In *Personal Places: Perspectives on Informal Art Environments*, ed. Daniel Franklin Ward, pp. 171-77. Bowling Green, Ohio: Bowling Green Univ. Popular Press, 1984.

Crow, Lester D., and Alice Crow. *Understanding Our Behavior: The Psychology of Personal and Social Adjustment*. New York: Alfred A. Knopf, 1956.

Csikszentmihalyi, Mihaly, and Eugene Rochberg-Halton. *The Meaning of Things: Domestic Symbols and the Self*. Cambridge: Cambridge University Press, 1981.

Dolgin, Janet, David S. Kemnitzer, and David M. Schneider. "As People Express Their Lives, So They Are. . . ." In *Symbolic Anthropology*, ed. Janet Dolgin, David S. Kemnitzer, and David M. Schneider, pp. 3-44. New York: Columbia University Press, 1977.

Dorson, Richard M. *Folkore and Fakelore: Essays Toward a Discipline of Folk Studies*. Cambridge: Harvard University Press, 1976.

Douglas, Mary. "Deciphering a Meal." In *Myth, Symbol, and Culture*, ed. Clifford Geertz, pp. 61-82. New York: W.W. Norton, 1971.

_____. *Implicit Meanings: Essays in Anthropology*. London: Routledge and Kegan Paul, 1975.

_____. *Natural Symbols: Explorations in Cosmology*. New York: Pantheon, 1982 ed.

Dundes, Alan. "Folk Ideas as Units of Worldview." *Journal of American Folklore* 84 (1971): 93-103.

_____. *Interpreting Folklore*. Bloomington: Indiana University Press, 1980.

Fleming, E. McClung. "Artifact Study: A Proposed Model." *Winterhur Portfolio*, ed. Ian M.G. Quimby, pp. 153-73. Charlottesville: University Press of Virginia, 1974.

Freud, Sigmund. *Civilization and Its Discontents*. New York: W.W. Norton, 1961.

_____. *Inhibitions, Symptoms, and Anxiety*. New York: W.W. Norton, 1977.

_____. *Introductory Lectures on Psychoanalysis*. New York: W.W. Norton, 1977.

Georges, Robert. "Toward an Understanding of Storytelling Events." *Journal of American Folklore* 82 (1969): 313-28.

_____. "Toward a Resolution of the Text/Context Controversy." *Western Folklore* 39 (1980): 34-40.

Georges, Robert A., and Michael Owen Jones. *People Studying People: The Human Element in Fieldwork*. Berkeley and Los Angeles: University of California Press, 1980.

Glassie, Henry. "Structure and Function, Folklore and the Artifact." *Semiotica* 7 (1973): 333-41.

_____. "The Variation of Concepts within Tradition: Barn Building in Otsego County, New York." *Geoscience and Man* 5 (1974): 177-235.

_____. *Folk Housing in Middle Virginia: A Structural Analysis of Historic Artifacts*. Knoxville: University of Tennessee Press, 1975.

Hanson, F. Allan, ed. *Studies in Symbolism and Cultural Communication*. Lawrence: University of Kansas Publications in Anthropology, Number 14, 1982.

Haselberger, Herta. "Method of Studying Ethnological Art." *Current Anthropology* 17 (1976): 687-701.

Jenkins, J. Geraint. "Field-Work and Documentation in Folk-Life Studies." *Journal of the Royal Anthropological Insititute* 90 (1960): 250-71.

Johnson, John M. *Doing Field Research*. New York: The Free Press, 1975.

Jones, Michael Owen. "Two Directions for Folkloristics in the Study of American Art." *Southern Folklore Quarterly* 32 (1968): 249-59.

_____. *The Hand Made Object and Its Maker.* Berkeley and Los Angeles: University of California Press, 1975.

_____. "A Feeling for Form, as Illustrated by People at Work." In *Folklore on Two Continents: Essays in Honor of Linda Dégh,* ed. Carl Lindahl and Nikolai Burlakoff, pp. 260-69. Bloomington, Indiana: Trickster Press, 1980.

Jung, Carl G. *The Symbolic Life.* Princeton, New Jersey: Princeton University Press, 1950.

_____. "Psychological Factors Determining Human Behavior." In Harvard Tercentenary Conference of Arts and Sciences, *Factors Determining Human Behavior,* pp. 49-63. 1937; reprint edition, New York: Arno Press, 1974.

Kaplan, Abraham. *The Conduct of Inquiry: Methodology for Behavioral Science.* Scranton: Chandler Publishing, 1964.

Ketner, Kenneth Laine. "The Role of Hypotheses in Folkloristics." *Journal of American Folklore* 86 (1973): 114-30.

Lévi-Strauss, Claude. "The Structural Study of Myth." In *Myth: A Symposium,* ed. Thomas A. Sebeok, pp. 81-106. Bloomington: Indiana University Press, 1958.

_____. *The Scope of Anthropology.* London: Jonathan Cape, 1967.

_____. *Structural Anthropology.* Garden City, New York: Doubleday, 1967.

Levitt, Eugene E. *The Psychology of Anxiety.* Indianapolis: Bobbs-Merrill, 1967.

Madan, T.N. "On Living Intimately with Strangers." In *Encounter and Experience: Personal Accounts of Fieldwork,* ed. André Béteille and T.N. Madan, pp. 135-56. Honolulu: University Press of Hawaii, 1975.

Malinowski, Bronislaw. *Coral Gardens and Their Magic.* 1935; reprint edition, New York: Dover Publications, 1978.

_____. "Culture as a Determinant of Behavior." In Harvard Tercentenary Conference of Arts and Sciences, *Factors Determining Human Behavior,* pp. 133-68. 1937; reprint edition, New York: Arno Press, 1974.

Maranda, Elli Köngas. "Individual and Tradition." *Studia Fennica* 20 (1976): 252-61.

Marks, Isaac M. *Living With Fear: Understanding and Coping with Anxiety.* New York: McGraw-Hill, 1978.

Mead, George Herbert. "What Social Objects Must Psychology Presuppose?" *Journal of Philosophy* 7 (1910): 174-80.

_____. "Social Consciousness and the Consciousness of Meaning." *The Psychological Bulletin* 7 (1910): 397-405.

_____. "A Behavioristic Account of the Significant Symbol." *Journal of Philosophy* 19 (1922): 157-63.

_____. "The Nature of Aesthetic Experience." *The International Journal of Ethics* 36 (1926): 382-93.

_____. *The Philosophy of the Present,* ed. Arthur E. Murphy. Chicago: University of Chicago Press, 1932.

_____. *On Social Psychology: Selected Papers,* ed. Anselm Strauss. Chicago: University of Chicago Press, 1964.

Nichols, John R. "How Opiates Change Behavior." *Scientific American* 212 (February 1965): 80-88.

_____. "The Homeostatic Reflex and Addictive Drugs." *Neurobehavioral Toxicology and Teratology* 5 (1983): 237-40.

Nicolaisen, Wilhelm. "Variant, Dialect, and Region: An Exploration in the Geography of Tradition." *New York Folklore* 6 (1980): 137-50.

Oring, Elliott. "Three Functions of Folklore: Traditional Functionalism as Explanation in Folkloristics." *Journal of American Folklore* 89 (1976): 67-80.

Prown, Jules David. "Mind in Matter: An Introduction to Material Culture Theory and Method." *Winterthur Portfolio* 17 (1982): 1-19.

Robbins, Michael C. "Material Culture and Cognition." In *Art and Aesthetics in Primitive Societies*, ed. Carol F. Jopling, pp. 328-34. New York: E.P. Dutton, 1971.

Roberts, Warren. "Fieldwork: Recording Material Culture." In *Folklore and Folklife: An Introduction*, ed. Richard M. Dorson, pp. 431-44. Chicago: University of Chicago Press, 1972.

Rosenberg, Bruce. "The Formula: New Directions?" *Folklore Preprint Series* 6, no. 4 (August 1978).

Segal, Dmitri. "Folklore Text and Social Context." *PTL: A Journal for Descriptive Poetics and Theory of Literature* 1 (1976): 367-82.

Sykes, Richard. "American Studies and the Concept of Culture: A Theory and Method." *American Quarterly* 15 (1963): 253-70.

Titon, Jeff Todd. "Every Day I Have the Blues: Improvisation and Daily Life." *Southern Folklore Quarterly* 42 (1978): 85-98.

_____. "The Life Story." *Journal of American Folklore* 93 (1980): 276-92.

Tokarew, S.A. "von einigen Aufgaben der ethnographischen Erforschung der materiellen Kultur." *Ethnologia Europaea* 6 (1972): 163-78.

Tyler, Stephen A., ed. *Cognitive Anthropology*. New York: Holt, Rinehart and Winston, 1969.

Wallace, Anthony F.C. *Culture and Personality*. New York: Random House, 1961.

Wax, Rosalie H. *Doing Fieldwork*. Chicago: University of Chicago Press, 1971.

Weiss, Albert Paul. *A Theoretical Basis of Human Behavior*. Columbus, Ohio: R.G. Adams, 1929.

Whiting, John W.M., and O.H. Mowrer. "Habit Progression and Regression." In *Personality in Nature, Society, and Culture*, ed. Clyde Kluckhohn and Henry Murray, pp. 315-24. New York: Alfred A. Knopf, 1948.

Wirth, Raymond. *Symbols: Public and Private*. Ithaca, New York: Cornell University Press, 1973.

FOLK CRAFT AND ART, AESTHETICS, AND CREATIVITY

A spotty record of writings is available to guide those curious about creativity's relation to folk culture, to our minds and bodies, and to gender. My pruned list emphasizes the bookshelf of traditional, material forms of creativity. It is an area of the library worth expanding.

Abrahams, Roger D. "Creativity, Individuality, and the Traditional Singer." *Studies in the Literary Imagination* 3 (1970): 5-34.

Adams, Marie Jeanne. "Afterword. Spheres of Men's and Women's Creativity." *Ethnologische Zeitschrift Zurich* 1 (1980): 163-67.

Alschuler, Rose H., and La Berta Haltwick. *Painting and Personality: A Study of Young Children.* Chicago: Univeristy of Chicago Press, 1969.

Ames, Kenneth L. "Folk Art: The Challenge and the Promise." In *Perspectives on American Folk Art,* ed. Ian M.G. Quimby and Scott T. Swank, pp. 293-324. New York: W.W. Norton, 1980.

Anderson, Harold, ed. *Creativity and Its Cultivation.* New York: Harper and Brothers, 1959.

Armstrong, Robert Plant. *The Affecting Presence: An Essay in Humanistic Anthropology.* Urbana: University of Illinois Press, 1971.

———. *The Powers of Presence: Consciousness, Myth, and Affecting Presence.* Philadelphia: University of Pennyslvania Press, 1981.

Barry, Herbert. "Relationships between Child Training and the Pictorial Arts." *Journal of Abnormal and Social Psychology* 54 (1957): 380-83.

Becker, Howard. "Art as Collective Action." *American Sociological Review* 30 (1974): 767-76.

Benton, Thomas Hart. *An Artist in America,* Fourth Revised Edition. Columbia: University of Missouri Press, 1983.

Boas, Franz. *Primitive Art.* 1927; reprint edition, New York: Dover Publications, 1955.

———. "Invention." In *General Anthropology,* ed. Franz Boas, pp. 238-81. Boston: D.C. Heath, 1938.

Bronner, Simon J. "The Durlauf Family: Three Generations of Stonecarvers in Southern Indiana." *Pioneer America* 12 (1980): 17-26.

———. "Investigating Identity and Expression in Folk Art." *Winterthur Portfolio* 16 (1981): 65-83.

———. "Manner Books and Suburban Houses: The Structure of Tradition and Aesthetics." *Winterthur Portfolio* 18 (1983): 61-68.

———. "The Anglo-American Aesthetic." In *Encyclopedia of Southern Culture,* ed. William Ferris and Charles Wilson. Chapel Hill: University of North Carolina Press, forthcoming.

Brown, J.A.C. *The Social Psychology of Industry .* 1954; reprint edition, New York: Penguin Books, 1980.

Camp, Charles, ed. *Traditional Craftsmanship in America: A Diagnostic Report.* Washington, D.C.: National Council for the Traditional Arts, 1983.

Culin, Stewart. "The Origin of Ornament." *Free Museum of Science and Art Bulletin* 2 (1900): 235-43.

———. "Creation in Art." *Brooklyn Museum Quarterly* 11 (1924): 91-100.

d'Azevedo, Warren L. "A Structural Approach to Esthetics: Toward a Definition of Art in Anthropology." *American Anthropologist* 60 (1958): 702-14.

Dewey, John. *Art as Experience.* New York: G.P. Putnam's Sons, 1934.

Dewhurst, C. Kurt, and Marsha MacDowell. *Rainbows in the Sky: The Folk Art of Michigan In the Twentieth Century.* East Lansing: Michigan State University, 1978.

Eaton, Allen, and Lucinda Crile. *Rural Handicrafts in the United States.* Washington D.C.: U.S. Department of Agriculture, 1946.

Fabian, Johannes, and Ilona Szombati-Fabian. "Folk Art from an Anthropological Perspective." In *Perspectives on American Folk Art,* ed. Ian M.G. Quimby and Scott T. Swank, pp. 247-92. New York: W.W. Norton, 1980.

Feintuch, Burt. "A Contextual and Cognitive Approach to Folk Art and Folk Craft." *New York Folklore* 2 (1976): 69-78.

Ferris, William. "Vision in Afro-American Folk Art: The Sculpture of James Thomas." *Journal of American Folklore* 88 (1975): 115-31.

Francis-Erhard, Doris. *Older Cleveland Folk Artists.* Cleveland: Department of Aging, n.d.

Glassie, Henry. "Folk Art." In *Folklore and Folklife: An Introduction,* ed. Richard M. Dorson, pp. 253-80. Chicago: University of Chicago Press, 1972.

Govenar, Alan. *Ohio Folk Traditions: A New Generation.* Lancaster, Ohio: Fairfield County District Library, 1981.

Hirsch, Susan E. *Roots of the American Working Class: The Industrialization of Crafts in Newark, 1800-1860.* Philadelphia: University of Pennsylvania Press, 1978.

Hirschfeld, Laurence A. "Art in Cunaland: Ideology and Cultural Adaptation." *Man* 12 (1977): 104-23.

Jones, Michael Owen. "Folk Art Production and the Folklorist's Obligation." *Journal of Popular Culture* 4 (1970): 194-212.

————. "The Concept of 'Aesthetic' in the Traditional Arts." *Western Folklore* 30 (1971): 77-104.

————. "Violations of Standards of Excellence and Preference in Utilitarian Art." *Western Folklore* 32 (1973): 19-32.

————. "L.A. Add-ons and Re-dos: Renovation in Folk Art and Architectural Design." In *Perspectives on American Folk Art,* ed. Ian M.G. Quimby and Scott T. Swank, pp. 325-64. New York: W.W. Norton, 1980.

————. "Modern Arts and Arcane Concepts: Expanding Folk Art Study." Paper read at Midwestern Conference on Folk Arts and Museums, Minneapolis, 1980.

Kouwenhoven, John A. *The Arts in Modern American Civilization.* New York: W.W. Norton, 1967.

Krause, Joseph H. *The Nature of Art.* Englewood Cliffs, New Jersey: Prentice-Hall, 1969.

Kris, Ernst, and Otto Kurz. *Legend, Myth, and Magic in the Image of the Artist.* New Haven: Yale University Press, 1979.

Kubler, George. "The Arts: Fine and Plain." In *Perspectives on American Folk Art,* ed. Ian M.G. Quimby and Scott T. Swank, pp. 234-46. New York: W.W. Norton, 1980.

MacDowell, Marsha, and C. Kurt Dewhurst. "Expanding Frontiers: The Michigan Folk Art Project." In *Perspectives on American Folk Art,* ed. Ian M.G. Quimby and Scott T. Swank, pp. 54-78. New York: W.W. Norton, 1980.

Mills, George. "Art: An Introduction to Qualitative Anthropology." In *Art and Aesthetics in Primitive Societies,* ed. Carol Jopling, pp. 73-98. New York: E.P. Dutton, 1971.

Munro, Thomas. *The Arts and Their Interrelations.* Cleveland: The Press of Case Western Reserve University, 1967.

Nickerson, Bruce. "Ron Thiesse, Industrial Folk Sculptor." *Western Folklore* 37 (1978): 128-33.

Ogden, Charles Kay. *Opposition: A Linguistic and Psychological Analysis.* Bloomington: Indiana University Press, 1967.

Reichard, Gladys A. "Craftsmanship and Folklore." *Journal of American Folklore* 53 (1940): 195-96.

Roberts, Warren. "Traditional Tools as Symbols: Some Examples from Indiana Tomb-stones." *Pioneer America* 12 (1980): 54-63.

Rogers, Carl R. "Toward a Theory of Creativity." In *Creativity and Its Cultivation,* ed. Harold H. Anderson, pp. 69-82. New York: Harper and Brothers, 1959.

Ross, Stephen David. "Some Ambiguities in Identifying the Work of Art." *Journal of Aesthetics and Art Criticism* 36 (1977): 137-46.

Sayers, Robert. "Traditional Southern Crafts in the Twentieth Century." In *Festival of American Folklife 1981,* ed. Jack Santino, pp. 17-19. Washington D.C.: Smithsonian Institution, 1981.

Schwartz, Ellen, Amy Snider and Don Sunseri, eds. *Images of Experience: Untutored Older Artists* New York: Pratt Institute, 1982.

Sklovskii, V. "Art as Technique." *Poetika* 3 (1919): 104-05.

Storr, Anthony. *The Dynamics of Creation.* New York: Atheneum, 1972.

Tolstoy, Leo. *What is Art? And Essays on Art.* Trans. Aylmer Maude. London: Oxford University Press, 1955.

Trillin, Calvin. "Simon Rodia: Watts Towers." *Naives and Visionaries,* pp. 21-31. (New York: E.P. Dutton and the Walker Art Center, Minneapolis, 1974).

Veblen, Thorstein. *The Instinct of Workmanship and the State of the Industrial Arts.* 1914 rpt.; Clifton, New Jersey: Augustus M. Kelley, 1964.

Vlach, John Michael. "American Folk Art: Questions and Quandaries." *Winterthur Portfolio* 15 (1980): 345-55.

————. *Charleston Blacksmith: The Life and Work of Philip Simmons.* Athens: University of Georgia Press, 1981.

Vygotsky, Lev Semenovich. *The Psychology of Art.* Cambridge: M.I.T. Press, 1971.

Whyte, Lancelot Law, ed. *Aspects of Form: A Symposium on Form in Nature and Art.* Bloomington: Indiana University Press, 1961.

Wilson, Eugene M. "Some Similarities between American and European Folk Houses." *Pioneer America* 3 (1971): 8-14.

————. "Form Changes in Folk Houses." *Geoscience and Man* 5 (1974): 65-71.

WOODCARVING AND CHAIN CARVING

Although you can readily find how-to and "art" books on woodcarving, few titles are studies of carvers or the communities in which they work. I chose titles for this selective list that either illustrate chain carvings and related forms, or provide technical, historical, and sociological information on woodcarving.

"A Whittler Champ." *Popular Science Monthly* (May 1927): 64.

Arnow, Harriette. *The Dollmaker.* 1954; reprint, New York: Avon, 1972.

Banks, Steven. *The Handicrafts of the Sailor.* New York: Arco Publishing, 1974.

Battiss, Walter W., G.W. Franz, J.W. Grossert, and H.P. Junod. *The Art of Africa.* Pietermaritzburg: Shuter and Shuter, 1958.

Bondhus, Will. "Carving a Ball Inside a Ball." *National Carvers Review* 9 (1978): 34-35.

Briggs, Charles. *The Wood Carvers of Córdova, New Mexico: Social Dimensions of an Artistic "Revival."* Knoxville: University of Tennessee Press, 1980.

Bronner, Simon J. "An Experiential Portrait of a Woodcarver." *Indiana Folklore* 13 (1980): 1-16.

_____. "The Folk Technics of Chain Carving." *Studies in Traditional American Crafts* 4 (1981): 3-19.

Christensen, Erwin. *Early American Wood Carving.* Cleveland and New York: The World Publishing Company, 1952.

Chulock, Vicki. "Folk Wood Carving and Related Wood Craft." Typescript, Indiana University Folklore Archives, 1968.

Clarke, Kenneth, and Ira Kohn. *Kentucky's Age of Wood.* Lexington: University Press of Kentucky, 1976.

Coats, Dale. "Seventy Years of Whittling." In *Central Oregon Folklife Festival,* ed. Suzi Jones, pp. 25-27. N.p., 1978.

Draper, John. "$1,000 in Cash Offered to Whittlers." *Popular Mechanics* (January 1932): 7-8.

Eaton, Allen H. *Handicrafts of the Southern Highlands.* 1937 reprint; New York: Dover Publications, 1973.

_____. *Handicrafts of New England.* New York: Harper and Row, 1949.

Evans, Len. *The Lore of the Love Spoon.* Cardiff, Wales: John Jones Cardiff Limited, 1978.

Faurot, Walter L. *The Art of Whittling.* Peoria, Illinois: The Manual Arts Press, 1930.

Galaune, P. *Medžio Dirbiniai I Knyga Lietuvių Liaudies Menas.* Vilnius:Valstybine Grozines Literaturos Leidykla, 1956.

Goodrich, Samuel G. *Recollections of a Lifetime,* 2 vols. New York: Miller, Orton and Mulligan, 1856.

Grier, Katherine C. *Celebrations in Wood: The Sculpture of John Scholl.* Harrisburg, Pennsylvania: William Penn Memorial Museum, 1979.

Hall, Julie. *The Sculpture of Fred Alten.* Detroit: Artrain, 1978.

Hansen, Bruce. "Local Artist Is Whittlin' While He Woodworks." *Indiana Daily Student* (25 April 1977): 12.

Harvest, William. "How to Whittle Interlocked Rings." *Popular Science Monthly* (December 1932): 70.

Hawthorne, Nathaniel. "Drowne's Wooden Image." In *The United States in Literature,* ed. Walter Blair, pp. 306-13. Glenview, Illinois: Scott, Foresman and Company, 1952.

"He's Been Whittling 45 Years: Dave Strausser, Wood Carver of Shoemakersville, Cuts Intricate Designs Out of Old Bed Posts." *The Evening* (Philadelphia), 17 July 1940.

Herrick, Mary S. "A Chenango County Coffin." *New York Folklore Quarterly* 8 (1952): 135-36.

Holme, Charles. *Peasant Art in Sweden, Lapland, and Iceland.* London: The Studio, 1910.

Houlton, Cecil W. *Whittling Wooden Variety Chains.* Monte Vista, Colorado: privately published, 1972.

Huehls, Patrick. "Lloyd Huehls: Whittling." Typescript, Indiana University Folklore Archives, 1972.

Johnstone, James B. *Woodcarving Techniques and Projects.* Menlo Park, California: Lane Publishing, 1971.

Jones, Gregory. "In North Carolina: Beware of Falling Cows." *Time* (18 April 1983): 12.

Jones, Suzi. *Oregon Folklore.* Eugene: Oregon Arts Commission, 1977.

Kaufman, Barbara Wahl. *A Sampling of Folk Art.* South Orange, New Jersey: Seton Hall University, 1983).

Klamkin, Marian, and Charles Klamkin. *Woodcarvings: North American Folk Sculptures.* New York: Hawthorn Books, 1974.

Lord, Priscilla Sawyer, and Daniel J. Foley. *The Folk Arts and Crafts of New England.* Philadelphia and New York: Chilton, 1965.

Mordoh, Alice Morrison. "Two Woodcarvers: Jasper, Dubois County, Indiana." *Indiana Folklore* 13 (1980): 17-29.

Morris, Ed. "Woodcarving: There's a Revival Underway." *Sky* (May 1980): 82-84.

Nadim, Asaad. "Testing Cybernetics in Khan-El-Khalili: A Study of Arabesque Carpenters." Ph.D. diss. Indiana University, 1975.

Parsons, Margaret Bouslough. "Floyd Cornell and Frank Hansel: Two Upstate Carvers." *New York Folklore* 1 (1975): 75-89.

Patterson, Nancy-Lou Gellermann. *Swiss-German and Dutch-German Mennonite Traditional Art in the Waterloo Region, Ontario.* Ottawa: National Museum of Man Mercury Series, Canadian Centre for Folk Culture Studies Paper No. 27, 1979.

Pawlowski, Robert. "Where's Your Knife?: The Disappearance of the Pocket Knife." *Mississippi Folklore Register* 13 (1979): 5-9.

Peña-Reyes, Myrna. "Wood Carving/Whittling by Loggers in Oregon, U.S.A." Typescript, Randall V. Mills Archives of Northwest Folklore, University of Oregon, 1973.

Pinto, Edward H. *Treen or Small Woodenware through the Ages.* London: B.T. Batsford, 1949.

————. *Treen and Other Bygones.* London: G. Bell and Sons, 1969.

Plath, Iona. *The Decorative Arts of Sweden.* New York: Charles Scribner's Sons, 1948.

Rawson, Marian Nicholl. *Candleday Art.* New York: E.P. Dutton, 1938.

Reuter, Frank. "John Arnold's Link Chains: A Study in Folk Art." *Mid-South Folklore* 5 (1977): 41-52.

Reese, Rosemary Sullivan. "Frank Moran: Woodcarver." M.A. thesis, State University of New York at Cooperstown, 1975.

"Skill and Perseverance." *Quarries and Mills* 1 (1930): 6.

Stewart, Janice S. *The Folk Arts of Norway.* New York: Dover, 1972.

Tangerman, E.J. *Whittling and Woodcarving.* 1936; reprint edition, New York: Dover, 1962.

————. *1001 Designs for Whittling and Woodcarving.* New York: McGraw Hill, 1976.

The Story of the Lovespoon. Swansea, Wales: Celtic Educational Limited, 1977.

Tilney, Philip V.R. *Artifacts from the CCFCS Collections.* Ottawa: National Museum of Man Mercury Series, Canadian Centre for Folk Culture Studies Paper No. 5, 1973.

Tschekalow, Alexander K. *Bauerliche russiche Holzkultur.* Dresden: VEB Verlag der Kunst, 1967.

Van Horn, Donald. *Carved in Wood: Folk Culture in the Arkansas Ozarks.* Batesville: Arkansas College Folklore Archive Publications, 1979.

Van Ravenswaay, Charles. *The Arts and Architecture of German Settlers in Missouri: A Vanishing Culture.* Columbia: University of Missouri Press, 1977.

Viires, A. *Woodworking in Estonia.* Jerusalem: Israel Program for Scientific Translations, 1969.

Vlach, John Michael. *The Afro-American Tradition in the Decorative Arts.* Cleveland: Cleveland Museum of Art, 1978.

Wiggins, William H. "The Wooden Chains That Bind: A Look at One Shared Creation of Two Diaspora Woodcarvers." In *Black People and Their Culture: Selected Writing from the African Diaspora*, ed. Linn Shapiro, pp. 29-32. Washington, D.C.: Smithsonian Institute, 1976.

AGING

The titles I list are principally studies and novels that particularly touch on cultural adaptation and folk arts. I would point to Barbara Myerhoff's work as an exemplary study and an influence on my research.

Achenbaum, W. Andrew. *Old Age in the New Land: The American Experience Since 1790*. Baltimore: The John Hopkins University Press, 1978.

Angrosino, M.V. "Anthropology and the Aged: A Preliminary Community Study." *The Gerontologist* 16 (1976): 174-80.

Atchley, Robert C. *The Social Forces in Later Life*. Belmont, California: Wadsworth Publishing, 1972.

————. *The Sociology of Retirement*. New York: John Wiley and Sons, 1976.

Binstock, Robert H., and Ethel Shanas, eds. *Handbook of Aging and the Social Sciences*. New York: Van Nostrand Reinhold, 1976.

Blau, Zena Smith. *Old Age in a Changing Society*. New York: New Viewpoints, 1973.

Brant, Sandra, and Elissa Cullman. *Small Folk: A Celebration of Childhood in America*. New York: E.P. Dutton, 1980.

Busse, Ewald, and Eric Pfeiffer, eds. *Behavior and Adaptation in Late Life*. Boston: Little, Brown and Company, 1969.

Clark, Margaret, and Barbara Gallatin Anderson. *Culture and Aging: An Anthropological Study of Older Americans*. Springfield, Illinois: Charles C. Thomas, 1967.

Cumming, Elaine, and William E. Henry. *Growing Old*. New York: Arno Press, 1979.

Dorson, Richard M. "Heart Disease and Folklore." In *Readings in American Folklore*, ed. Jan Harold Brunvand, pp. 124-37. New York: W.W. Norton, 1979.

Fine, Gary Alan. "Children and Their Culture: Exploring Newell's Paradox." *Western Folklore* 39 (1980): 170-83.

Fischer, David Hackett. *Growing Old in America*. New York: Oxford University Press, 1977.

Fontana, Andrea. *The Last Frontier: The Social Meaning of Growing Old*. Beverly Hills: Sage Publications, 1977.

Gubrium, Jaber F. *The Myth of the Golden Years: A Socio-Environmental Theory of Aging*. Springfield, Illinois: Charles C. Thomas, 1973.

Hendricks, Jon, ed. *Being and Becoming Old*. Farmingdale, New York: Baywood Publishing, 1980.

Huxley, Aldous. *Point Counter Point*, Modern Library ed., New York: Doubleday Doran, 1928.

Jabbour, Alan, "Some Thoughts from a Folk Cultural Perspective." In *Perspectives on Aging*. ed. Priscilla W. Johnston, pp. 139-49. Cambridge, Massachusetts: Ballinger, 1982.

Kastenbaum, Robert, ed. *New Thoughts on Old Age*. New York: Springer Publishing, 1964.

Knapp, Mary, and Herbert Knapp. *One Potato, Two Potato . . . The Secret Education of American Children.* New York: W.W. Norton, 1976.

Myerhoff, Barbara. *Number Our Days.* New York: Simon and Schuster, 1978.

Myerhoff, Barbara, and Andrei Simic. *Life's Career—Aging: Cultural Variations in Growing Old.* Beverly Hills: Sage Publications, 1977.

Neugarten, Bernice L., ed. *Middle Age and Aging: A Reader in Social Psychology.* Chicago: University of Chicago Press, 1968.

Reichard, Suzanne, Florine Livson, and Paul Petersen. *Aging and Personality: A Study of Eighty-Seven Older Men.* New York: John Wiley, 1962.

Riley, Matilda White. *Aging from Birth to Death: Interdisciplinary Perspectives.* Boulder, Colorado: Westview Press, 1979.

Rose, Arnold, and Warren Peterson. *Older People and Their Social World: The Sub-Culture of the Aging.* Philadelphia: F.A. Davis, 1965.

Rosenberg, George S. *The Worker Grows Old.* San Francisco: Jossey-Bass, 1970.

Rowles, Graham D. *Prisoners of Space; Exploring the Geographical Experience of Older People.* Boulder, Colorado: Westview Press, 1978.

Simmons, Leo W. *The Role of the Aged in Primitive Society.* New Haven:Yale University Press, 1945.

Snider, Amy Brook. "The Education of the Elderly Artist." In *Images of Experience: Untutored Older Artists,* ed. Ellen Schwartz, Amy Snider, and Don Sunseri, pp. 2-6. New York: Pratt Institute, 1982.

Spicker, Stuart F.; Kathleen Woodward, and David D. van Tassel, eds. *Aging and the Elderly: Humanistic Perspectives.* Atlantic Highlands, New Jersey: Humanities Press, 1978.

Tibbits, Clark. "The Future of Research in Social Gerontology." In *Age with a Future,* ed. Per From Hansen. Copenhagen: Munksgaard, 1964.

Tibbits, Clark, and Wilma Donahue. *Social and Psychological Aspects of Aging.* New York: Columbia University Press, 1962.

Wan, Thomas T.H. *Stressful Life Events, Social Support Networks, and Gerontological Health.* Lexington: Lexington Books, D.C. Heath, 1982.

Weber, Barbara. "Folk Art Therapy with a Group of Old People." *American Journal of Art Therapy* 20 (1981): 47-52.

Wright, H. Beric. *Solving the Problems of Retirement.* London: Institute of Directors, 1968.

Youmans, E. Grant, ed. *Older Rural Americans: A Sociological Perspective.* Lexington: University of Kentucky Press, 1967.

PLAY, RITUAL, BELIEF, AND RIDDLING

The categories of play, ritual, belief, and riddling have a direct relation to the study of art. The following trimmed list contains works in these categories that informed my research and could inform similar types of material culture study.

Abrahams, Roger D. "The Literary Study of the Riddle." *Texas Studies in Literature and Language* 14 (1972): 177-97.

————. "Rituals in Culture." *Folklore Preprint Series,* 5, no. 1. Bloomington, Indiana: Folklore Publications Group, n.d.

_____. *Between the Living and the Dead.* Helsinki: Academia Scientiarum Fennica, FF Communications No. 225, 1980.

Abrahams, Roger D., and Alan Dundes. "Riddles." In *Folklore and Folklife: An Introduction,* ed. Richard M. Dorson, pp. 129-43. Chicago: University of Chicago Press, 1972.

Bauman, Richard, and Joel Sherzer, eds. *Explorations in the Ethnography of Speaking.* New York: Cambridge University Press, 1974.

Bell, Michael Edward. "Pattern, Structure, and Logic in Afro-American Hoodoo Performance." Ph.D. diss., Indiana University, 1980.

Ben-Amos, Dan. "Solutions to Riddles." *Journal of American Folklore* 89 (1976): 249-54.

Csikszentmihalyi, Mihaly. *Beyond Boredom and Anxiety.* San Francisco: Jossey-Bass, 1975.

_____. "Some Paradoxes in the Definition of Play." In *Play as Context,* ed. A.T. Cheska, pp. 14-26. New York: Leisure Press, 1981.

Davies, Robertson. "A Few Kind Words for Superstition." *Newsweek* (20 November 1978): 23.

Dundes, Alan, and Carl Pagter. *Work Hard and You Shall Be Rewarded: Urban Folklore from the Paperwork Empire.* Bloomington: Indiana University Press, 1978.

Evans, David. "Riddling and the Structure of Context." *Journal of American Folklore* 89 (1976): 166-88.

Georges, Robert A., and Alan Dundes. "Toward A Structural Definition of the Riddle." *Journal of American Folklore* 76 (1963): 111-18.

Hamnett, Ian. "Ambiguity, Classification and Change: The Function of Riddles." *Man* 2 (1967): 379-92.

Hand, Wayland D. "Folk Belief and Superstition: A Crucial Field of Folklore Long Neglected." In *Folklore Today: A Festschrift for Richard M. Dorson,* ed. Linda Dégh, Henry Glassie, and Felix J. Oinas, pp. 209-20. Bloomington: Indiana University, 1976.

Hufford, David J. *The Terror That Comes in the Night: An Experience-Centered Study of Supernatural Assault Traditions.* Philadelphia: University of Pennsylvania Press, 1982.

Huizinga, Johan. *Homo Ludens: A Study of the Play Element in Culture.* Boston: The Beacon Press, 1955.

Ketner, Kenneth L. "Superstitious Pigeons, Hydrophobia, and Conventional Wisdom." *Western Folklore* 30 (1971): 1-18.

Kirshenblatt-Gimblett, Barbara, ed. *Speech Play: Research and Resources for the Study of Linguistic Creativity.* Philadelphia: University of Pennsylvania Press, 1976.

Lieber, Michael D. "Riddles, Cultural Categories, and World View." *Journal of American Folklore* 89 (1976): 255-65.

Maranda, Elli Köngäs. "Riddles and Riddling: An Introduction." *Journal of American Folklore* 89 (1976): 127-38.

McDowell, John Holmes. *Children's Riddling.* Bloomington: Indiana University Press, 1979.

Moore, Danny W. "The Deductive Riddle: An Adaptation to Modern Society." *North Carolina Folklore* 22 (1974): 119-25.

Mergen, Bernard. *Play and Playthings: A Reference Guide.* Westport, Connecticut: Greenwood Press, 1982.

Nusbaum, Philip. "A Conversational Approach to Occupational Folklore: Conversation, Work, Play, and the Workplace." *Folklore Forum* 11 (1978): 18-28.

Office of Folklife Programs and Renwick Gallery of the National Museum of Art. *Celebration: A World of Art and Ritual.* Washington, D.C.: Smithsonian Institution Press, 1982.

Radar, Edmond. "A Genealogy: Play, Folklore, and Art." *Diogenes* no. 103 (Fall 1978): 78-99.

Scott, Charles T. "On Defining the Riddle: The Problem of a Structural Unit." In *Folklore Genres*, ed. Dan Ben Amos, pp. 77-90. Austin: University of Texas Press, 1976.

Sutton-Smith, Brian. "A Developmental Psychology of Play and the Arts." *Perspectives on Education* (Spring 1971): 8-17.

————. "Toys for Object and Role Mastery." In *Educational Toys in America: 1800 to the Present*, ed. Karen Hewitt and Louise Roomet, pp. 11-25. Burlington, Vermont: Fleming Museum, University of Vermont, 1979.

Turner, Victor, ed. *Celebration: Studies in Festivity and Ritual.* Washington, D.C.: Smithsonian Insitution Press, 1982.

Turner, Victor. *The Ritual Process: Structure and Anti-Structure.* Chicago: Aldine, 1969.

————. *Dramas, Fields and Metaphors: Symbolic Action in Human Society.* Ithaca: Cornell University Press, 1974.

————. "Liminality and the Performative Genres." In *Studies in Symbolism and Cultural Communication*, ed. F. Allan Hanson, pp. 25-41.

Index

Abrahams, Roger (folklorist), 109
Adams, Marie Jeanne (anthropologist), 153
adjustment: to changes, 28-30; to emotional stress, 35; to urbanization, 64-65; through woodcarving, 57, 127; to retirement, 139
Adyeville, Indiana, 1, 22
aging: and regression-progression behavioral complex, 131; and impotence, 139-40; as a career, 140, 146; and change, 152. See also retirement
Ames, Kenneth (historian), 70
anxiety: reduced by chain carving, 127; chains as projection of, 136
architecture: and witchcraft, 26-27; folk, as mediator, 97
Armstrong, Jack, 76
Armstrong, Robert Plant, 110
Arnow, Harriette: The Dollmaker, 67-68
art: woodcarving as, 102-05, 113; and play, 153
audience of chain carvers. See viewers

ball and chain, 41
banjo-playing, 19-20
Banks, Steven, 13
baseball, 28
Bennett, Dorothy (wife of Earnest): and quilting, 67, 107; and chain bracelet, 106
Bennett, Earnest, 9-10; repertoire of carvings, 9, 74, 81, 91, 106, 116-18,

120, 124; work areas, 19, 80; Earnest's story, 59-67; aesthetic decisions of, 96; on involvement in wood carving, 97; social carving of, 101-02; demonstrations and exhibitions by, 106-07, 132, 147; letter from, 147; mention 14, 20, 67, 68, 70, 71, 75, 96, 115-16, 128, 140, 143, 151
Bennington, Delpha (wife of Floyd), 46-47, 51-52
Bennington, Floyd, 4-5; repertoire of carvings, 4-7, 74-75, 116, 125; Floyd's story, 42-52; birth of, 43; retirement of, 47, 128; use of pocketknife by, 76; work areas of, 80; woods used by, 80; on aesthetics, 98; on art, 103-05; as teacher emeritus, 146-47; mention, 14, 20, 67, 71, 96, 115-16, 127-28, 135-36, 140-41, 143, 156
Bennington, John (brother of Floyd), 43
Bennington, Virgil (brother of Floyd), 43
Benton, Thomas Hart (painter), 35-36
Best Little Whorehouse in Texas, The (film), 147
bilateral symmetry, 88
blacksmith as craftsman, 28
blades, pocketknife, 77
Blemker, Ike, 14
Blemker, Lil, 3, 14, 21; and carved chain, 105; and carved pig, 125
Blume, Casper (grandfather of George), 22, 37

"*Chain Carvers* offers not only a new and more revealing treatment of chain carvers and carving but also is the most fully developed examination of folk art as a psychological phenomenon and an index to psychic states and processes"—Michael Owen Jones.

Chains carved out of a single block of wood, cages whittled with wooden balls rattling inside—all "made with just a pocketknife"—are among our most enduring folk designs. Who makes them and why? What is their history? What do they mean—for their makers, for their viewers, for our society?

Simon Bronner found chain carvers among old men in southern Indiana—men transplanted from the country landscape where they grew up to industrial towns. Retired, they took up a skill they remembered from childhood. Bronner learned that to talk about traditional woodcarving today is to talk about aging and masculinity, about social and economic change, but mostly about the carvers themselves and the craft they hold dear.

Four men—George Blume, Floyd Bennington, Wandley Burch, and Earnest Bennett—were at the center of Bronner's study. He discovered how creativity helped them adjust to change, and how viewers' responses to their carving revealed background and worldview. In recording the narratives of the men's lives, the folk stories, anecdotes, and sayings that laced their conversation, and their accounts of the aesthetics and techniques of their work, Bronner finds new insight into the creativity impulse and the functions and symbolism of traditional crafts.